Praise for *Drunk from the Bitter Truth*

"[Margolin's] poems have a powerfully contemporary ring, dealing with spiritual identity, sensuality and depression."
— *Na'amat Woman*

"Margolin's persona poems, including those about the biblical Mary, show the range of her talent and her ability to bring the world of others to her readers; hopefully this volume will gain her an even wider audience."
— *Lilith*

"Shirley Kumove's assiduous research, profound knowledge of Yiddish, and poetic sensibilities combine to make this a valuable and desirable contribution to the library of translated texts."
— Barbara Harshav, cotranslator of
American Yiddish Poetry: A Bilingual Anthology

"This bilingual edition makes available an important body of Yiddish poetry by a major author whose concerns remain relevant today."
— Ken Frieden, editor and cotranslator of
Classic Yiddish Stories of S. Y. Abramovitsh,
Sholem Aleichem, and I. L. Peretz

"*Drunk from the Bitter Truth* is a welcome addition to the growing body of Yiddish literature published bilingually. All nuances of Margolin's complex poetry are reflected in Kumove's precise, coherent, and eloquent translation."
— Anna Shternshis, University of Toronto

DRUNK FROM THE BITTER TRUTH

Anna Margolin

SUNY series, Women Writers in Translation

Marilyn Gaddis Rose, Editor

drunk from the bitter truth

the poems of **A n n a M a r g o l i n**

TRANSLATED

EDITED

AND WITH AN

INTRODUCTION BY

Shirley Kumove

State University of New York Press

Lider [Poems] by Anna Margolin (New York, 1929)
English translations © 1995, 1996, 1997, 1998, 2001, 2002, 2005 by Shirley Kumove.
Introduction, notes, and biographical notes © 2005 by Shirley Kumove.
Some of these translations first appeared in the following journals:
"My Ancestors Speak," "Brisk (Brest-Litovsk)," "Drunk from the Bitter Truth,"
"Full of Night and Weeping," "Among the Chinese Lanterns," "Mary Wants to Be a
Beggar Woman," "I Want Angry and Tender One": *Writ Magazine,* 1995
"You": *Prism International,* 1996
"Drunk On the Bitter Truth," "A Woman Says," "All Mute Things Speak Today,"
"Untitled (All Mute Things Speak Today):" *Two Lines,* 1997
"What Do You Want, Mary?" "Her Smile," "Just Like My Tearful Gaze," "The Gangster,"
"Beautiful Words of Marble and Gold," "In the Streets": *Metamorphoses,* 1998
"Full of Night and Weeping," "Drunk from the Bitter Truth," "My Ancestors
Speak": *Parchment,* 2001
"My Ancestors Speak," "Full of Night and Weeping": *Five Fingers Review,* 2002

Photograph of Anna Margolin courtesy of YIVO Archives.
Photograph of Anna Margolin's gravestone, page xxxiii, courtesy of Sarah Swartz.
Drawing by Gail Geltner used with permission.

Published by
STATE UNIVERSITY OF NEW YORK PRESS, ALBANY

© 2005 Shirley Kumove

For information, contact State University of New York Press, Albany, NY
www.sunypress.edu

Production, Laurie Searl
Marketing, Anne M. Valentine

Library of Congress Cataloging-in-Publication Data
Margolin, Anna.
    [Poems. English & Yiddish]
    Drunk from the bitter truth : the poems of Anna Margolin / Anna Margolin ; edited,
translated, and an introduction by Shirley Kumove.
        p.   cm. -- (SUNY series, women writers in translation)
    English and Yiddish.
    Includes the work Lider and a supplement of poems printed in daily newspapers after
Lider was published.
    Includes bibliographical references and indexes.
    ISBN 978-0-7914-6579-0 (hc. alk. paper)—978-0-7914-6580-6 (pbk. alk. paper)
        I. Kumove, Shirley, 1931– . II. Title III. Series.
    PJ5129.MS125A24   2005
    839'.113—dc22   2004065682

10   9   8   7   6   5   4   3   2   1

This work was undertaken following the
tragic death of my beloved granddaughter

Merav Sarah Kumove z"l
1979–1989

and it is lovingly dedicated to her memory

Cautiously I carry
your voices, smiles, grimaces
through raw, rushing streets
as one carries a song on one's lips,
or a costly ring on one's finger.

contents

acknowledgments

I want to express my deep appreciation to Roger Greenwald, poet and translator. In addition to his meticulous reading of the entire manuscript and his trenchant comments, he has been an invaluable guide and mentor.

To Dr. Avraham Novershtern, Professor of Yiddish Literature, Hebrew University, Jerusalem, with whom I had the pleasure of studying Women in Yiddish Literature at the National Yiddish Book Center in Amherst, Mass., and to whom I am indebted for the supplementary poems; his Yiddish edition of the poems of Anna Margolin published by Magnes Press, Jerusalem, 1991, has been valuable to me.

To Dr. Alex Page, Professor Emeritus of English Literature, University of Massachussetts; Henia and Nokhem Reinhartz; and Brina Menachovsky Rose. Each of them undertook a careful reading of the entire text and offered suggestions for improvement of both style and content. Their criticism and encouragement contributed greatly to the final version.

Dr. Anita Norich, Professor of English Literature, University of Michigan, Ann Arbor, whose discussions at Klez Kamp, sponsored by YIVO, New York, first sparked insight into the poetry of Anna Margolin; Shirley Hochhausen and Sheva Zucker, who provided insight into several poems; Clare Recht, for her useful comments on the introductory material; Rhea Tregebov, who edited an earlier version of the introduction and whose suggestions helped refine the text; and Dr. Ellen Kellman, Lecturer in Yiddish, Brandeis University, for providing helpful research material.

For earlier translations of various poems by Anna Margolin, I thank Adrienne Cooper, Marcia Falk, Kathryn Hellerstein, and Ruth Whitman. Their work informed and clarified my own approach. My translation of "Slender Ships" turned out to be identical to that of Marcia Falk's. I was not aware of this at the time; when I discovered it, I decided it would be pointless to alter my version merely for the sake of being different.

My thanks to the editors of the following journals where earlier versions of poems in this collection appeared: *Writ 27, Prism International, Two Lines, Metamorphoses, Parchment,* and *Five Fingers Review.*

I am grateful to the National Yiddish Book Center for providing me with a copy of the original volume of Anna Margolin's book of poems. The YIVO Archives made Margolin's papers available to me.

I wish also to express my appreciation to the Yiddish Women Writers Study Group of Toronto, of which I was a member. This group dedicated itself to rediscovering long-neglected works by Yiddish women writers and I had the privilege of working with them on the stories that became the book *Found Treasures.* I am grateful to Sarah Swartz for first bringing to my attention the writings of Anna Margolin, and to her and Frieda Forman for sharing research material about her. I brought a number of translations to the group as works in progress, and I am indebted to my colleagues for clarification of difficult words and phrases, as well as suggestions for improvement.

The drawing on page xxxix courtesy of Toronto artist Gail Geltner, is taken from her book *What You See: Drawings by Gail Geltner,* published by Second Story Press, Toronto, 1992.

My heartfelt thanks to my husband, Aryeh, for the depth of his Jewish knowledge, his intuitive understanding of the poetry of Anna Margolin, his critical acumen, and his steadfast advice and encouragement.

introduction: the poetry of ANNA MARGOLIN

HER LIFE AND TIMES

Anna Margolin's reputation rests on one slim volume of Yiddish poetry published in New York City in 1929. Her poetry remains remarkably fresh and contemporary in spite of having been written a long time ago: the language is original and personal, and her themes of anxiety, loneliness, and search for identity and meaning are, if anything, more relevant today than they were in her lifetime. To enter a Margolin poem is to accompany a distinguished and imaginative mind that has set out on an unpredictable journey. In some poems, Margolin uses favourite images to present observations; in others she goes much deeper, searching to define her own worth and in the process creating powerful lyric and meditative works.

Anna Margolin described her poetic mission in the first epitaph she wrote:

> Say this: until her death
> She faithfully protected
> With her bare hands
> The flame entrusted to her
> And in that same fire
> She burned.

This is the essence of her brief, creative career and is central to understanding her existential dilemma. Anna Margolin had a kind of double vision that enabled her to stand outside herself and observe her artistic persona. This double vision, which animates her poetry, recalls the portraits by Picasso in which the face is carved in sharp planes and the eyes are focused in separate directions. Gustave Flaubert once characterized the artist as a disease of society, and Franz Kafka, in a variation on this theme, claimed that poetry is disease. If one reads this word as dis-ease, it may fairly be applied to Anna Margolin. Restless and dislocated, Margolin was deeply at odds with the world in which she found herself.

xiii

Most of what we know about Anna Margolin comes from a memoir, *fun undzer friling*[1] (From Our Springtime), written by the Yiddish poet Reuven Ayzland, her companion for the last thirty years of her life, and from an exchange of more than two hundred letters between them found in the Margolin Collection of the YIVO Archives in New York. Although Ayzland's memoir is filtered through his personal perceptions, he does give us a picture of her early life, the influences that formed her personality and artistic vision, and the mental and physical deterioration that followed the publication of her book.

Anna Margolin was born Rosa Lebensboym in Brisk (Brest-Litovsk), White Russia (Belarus) in 1887. The late nineteenth and early twentieth centuries were a period of enormous change and profound ferment in Jewish life. What had once been the fairly orderly life of the Eastern European Jewish communities was rent by increasingly divisive forces, and the traditional social fabric steadily weakened. At the same time, the growing number of pogroms and outrages against Jews, combined with economic deprivation, forced a large-scale exodus of Jews from Eastern Europe to safer havens in North America and elsewhere.

When Rosa Lebensboym was born, Jews in Eastern Europe were struggling with the *haskole* (Jewish Enlightenment) that was sweeping through the Jewish communities and bringing forces of modernism and secularism in their wake. This struggle was reflected within her own family. Her father Menakhem was an enlightened grain merchant, both pious and knowledgeable in worldly subjects; her mother Dvoyre Leye was an unsophisticated woman, traditional in outlook and uncomprehending of the social forces swirling around her. The new ideas held out the promise of freedom, equality, and fraternity for Jewish men in a wider society, but for many of their wives, it offered only dislocation and tragic loss. This was the spirit of the age into which Rosa Lebensboym was born and in which she was raised.

Rosa was precocious and an only child. An apt and diligent student, she studied at *gymnasium* (uncommon for Jewish girls of that time) and was also tutored at home in Jewish subjects and in European languages. She was strikingly beautiful, extremely well-read, and by the age of fifteen, fully developed as a woman. She had thick ash-blonde hair that fell

---

1. Reuven Ayzland, *Fun undzer friling* (From Our Springtime) (New York: Farlag Inzl, 1954), pp. 129–172.

to her knees, large blue eyes, and a musical voice. She was well aware of her sexual appeal and enjoyed youthful flirtations and love affairs.

Rosa Lebensboym came to New York for the first time in 1906 at the age of eighteen to prepare herself for university entrance. She had been sent to America because her father wanted to break up his head-strong daughter's current love affair. However, instead of enrolling in university as planned, she quickly became immersed in the intellectual life of the Lower East Side. Soon after, she began a tempestuous but short-lived love affair with a man many years her senior, Chaim Zhitlowsky—a Yiddish author, a theoretician of Jewish nationalism, socialism, and radical secularism, and a charismatic orator. Around this time, she wrote short stories that appeared in journals under a variety of pseudonyms.

By the time Rosa settled permanently in America in 1913 at the age of twenty-six, she had already traveled extensively—from her place of birth, Brisk (Brest-Litovsk), to Koenigsburg, Warsaw, and Odessa. She had spent two years in New York, visited London and Paris, returned to Warsaw, and spent two years in Palestine. At that time, such an itinerary was unusual for a woman of her age and status. Her travels included meetings with leading anarchists in London and Paris and a short-lived marriage in Warsaw to the writer Moshe Stavsky.

After the breakup of her marriage to Stavsky, with whom she had migrated to Palestine, she left her infant son Naaman in the permanent care of his father and returned to New York. She never saw her son again and, according to Reuven Ayzland, never spoke of him. We can only surmise the effect this separation had on her, since this chapter of her life remains obscure and she made no overt reference to it in her poetry. Ayzland relates that she kept a hidden photograph of herself with her infant son in her lap; he relates an incident in which she became hysterical and physically ill when she chanced upon this photograph.

When Rosa Lebensboym returned to New York in 1913, she became a columnist for the women's section of the recently founded Yiddish daily newspaper *Der Tog* (The Day). She wrote a weekly column called "In the Woman's World" under her real name and for a time, she was also a member of the editorial board of that newspaper. When she began publishing poetry in 1920, she took the name Anna Margolin, the name she used for the rest of her life.

Anna Margolin was an exceptionally beautiful and gifted woman, fiercely individualistic and with a volatile temperament, who lived a tempestuous, unconventional life. Like many other Jewish women writers—Clare Goll (Franco-German poet, 1901–1977), Elsa Lasker Schüler (German poet, 1869–1945), and Yente Serdatsky (Yiddish writer, 1877–1962)—she adopted a bohemian and an eccentric lifestyle. A complex personality torn by fundamental tensions, Margolin had a keen wit, intellectual acumen, and uncompromising honesty; she was also high-strung and aggressively self-confident. She threw herself into both intellectual pursuits and romantic attachments with great passion and had a succession of lovers beyond her two marriages. Most of her liaisons were with exceptional and prominent men.

In America, Margolin married in 1917 for the second time, to Hirsh Leyb Gordon, a successful journalist five years her junior, who later became a psychiatrist. While she was still living with him in New Haven, Connecticut, the Yiddish poet Reuven Ayzland kept her informed about how her poems were being received in the New York cafés where the Yiddish literary intelligentsia gathered. About the reception of her poem "To Be a Beggarwoman," which had just appeared in the weekly newspaper, *Di Fraye Arbeter Shtime* (The Liberated Workers' Voice), he wrote:

> Last night, Anna Margolin was the main topic among the literati. A thousand hypotheses were offered about who might be hiding behind the name, and the general opinion is that *it must certainly be a man.* (My emphasis.)

Later, he wrote her again:

> Why people want Anna Margolin to be a man is beyond me. The general opinion, however, is that these poems are written by an experienced hand. And *a woman can't write like that.* (My emphasis.) [2]

These clearly prejudiced responses indicate how widespread such attitudes were at that time and perhaps cast some light on the reception her book was to receive.

In 1919 she formed a relationship with Reuven Ayzland, who was also married, which endured for the rest of her life. In his memoir, Ayzland claimed that her threats of suicide forced him into a bitter divorce.

---

2. Avraham Novershtern, "Anna Margolin—Materialn tsu ir poetisher geshtalt" (Correspondence between Anna Margolin and Reuven Ayzland), *YIVO Bleter,* Vol. 1, 1991, p. 151.

His children became permanently estranged from him, and when he died they destroyed his papers. Whether Ayzland and Margolin married is not clear, but they lived together as husband and wife for thirty years. In a letter to him, Margolin wrote:

> I love you very much. You are kneaded into my life but remarkably not into me. I am alone. Inside, I am so alone and so free as not even to know you. I am a woman with a lot of cynicism and sinful curiosity. . . .
>
> I hate my contrived, artificial pride and those other characteristics of mine which did not allow me to make a move out of the little picture frame into which I had placed myself.[3]

In the early twentieth century, when Anna Margolin began her career, modern Yiddish literature did not yet have much of a literary tradition. Up to that point, Jewish culture and literature were focused primarily on the study of the Bible and the Talmud in the original Hebrew and Aramaic. This was essentially a male activity. Yiddish was the spoken language of everyday life, and Yiddish literature consisted mainly of folk tales and religious tracts for uneducated men and for women and children. In a society in which study of the Bible was commonplace, even a comprehensive Yiddish literary translation of the Bible did not appear until the twentieth century.

Yiddish made the leap from rather unsophisticated narratives and prayers to a modern literature without any transitional stages. This leap was inspired by the *Haskole* (Jewish Enlightenment) and spurred on by the emergence of modern secular Hebrew literature in the nineteenth century. Two of the earliest modern Yiddish writers, Mendele Mokher-Sforim and Sholem Aleichem, began their literary careers writing in Hebrew, but soon turned to Yiddish because it had a larger base of readers. Yiddish literature was part of the ferment in Jewish life in Eastern Europe, where Jews were emerging from passive acceptance of tradition into more active roles in education, politics, and religion.

This change, and the accompanying social turmoil, was reflected in Yiddish literature. In one generation Yiddish blossomed in the whole range of modern genres—novels, short stories, poetry, essays,

---

3. Novershtern, "Anna Margolin—Materialn tsu ir poetisher geshtalt," p. 161.

and journalism. But although Yiddish was the spoken language at home and on the street, early Yiddish writers could acquire no formal education, because Yiddish-language schools didn't emerge until after World War I. Few Yiddish dictionaries and grammars were available, and there were hardly any literary models from earlier generations to emulate or from which to depart. The first Yiddish writers, both men and women, were in effect literary orphans, as Abraham Novershtern so aptly calls them. They had to supplement such education as they had by reading books in other languages. Their style was heavily influenced by European Romantic and Classical poetry, Russian symbolism, German Expressionism, and Post-Expressionism, but the very lack of any literary tradition in modern Yiddish poetry, as well as experimentation with foreign poetic forms, may well have been a liberating force.

The Yiddish literary and intellectual world of the Lower East Side that Anna Margolin entered was male-dominated and fiercely competitive. It was not kind to Yiddish women writers and treated them as minor contributors. This world was mainly focused on the Yiddish newspapers and on the cafés where the intelligentsia gathered to debate the merits of recently published editorials, essays, poems, and short stories. Ruth Wisse[4] suggests that the café debates were modeled on the debates in the *yeshivahs* where most of the men had received their early training. They had thrown off the yoke of religious observance, but they transplanted to a secular setting in North America the habits of close textual analysis and highly charged argument supported by citation of relevant passages.

Few women published in Yiddish before World War I, but afterward there was a sudden outburst of literary activity by women writing in Yiddish in Kiev, Lodz, New York, and other centers. Poetry was the leading genre for literary experimentation in Yiddish writing, particularly in New York, and women fit easily into this trend. The Canadian Yiddish novelist Chava Rosenfarb claims that women mainly wrote poetry and short stories because their domestic duties did not allow them the leisure to devote to longer pieces of fiction, but one may suspect that poetry lent itself more readily to the expression of long-suppressed emotions too intense for prose. Chava Rosenfarb points out that the women writers:

---

4. Ruth R. Wisse, *A Little Love in Big Manhattan* (Cambridge: Harvard University Press, 1988), p. 4.

were far more candid and outspoken than their male counter-parts. They shed the fig leaves of false modesty and cele-brated their feminine sensuality.[5]

Many of the literati were unable to deal with the new breed of woman, who shared their interest in literature and politics and could hold their own in an intellectual argument. In her youth, Anna Margolin was an active member of a socialist organization, but later she withdrew from political action to devote herself entirely to literature. Neverthe-less, she remained well-informed about economic and political affairs. The critics characterized women writers as emotional and sentimental, compared them only to each other, and considered their work unworthy of examination as part of the larger body of modern Yiddish literature.

In the first decade of the twentieth century, when Margolin re-turned to America, New York City was becoming the liveliest and most populous Jewish center in the world. From a single Yiddish newspaper with a circulation of under 4,000 in 1887, the Yiddish press in New York grew to consist of five dailies with a circulation of more than 500,000 by 1915. These Yiddish newspapers were a major avenue for the dissemination of fiction, poetry, and literary criticism. They pub-lished the work of the most important writers, providing them with jobs as journalists and editors and a forum in which to expound their opinions on subjects ranging from culture to Jewish history, literature, politics, and world events.

The Yiddish newspapers, however, provided only limited opportu-nities for female writers. These women did not write about economics or politics, but were invariably consigned to the other side of the *mekhitse* (the barrier separating men from women in the synagogue)—to the women's pages, where they were limited to writing about fashion, home decor, and child rearing. Many of them, including Anna Margolin, resented this restriction. In addition to a weekly column, Margolin wrote fiction and essays. Most of these pieces appeared under her real name, Rosa Lebensboym, although many of her earlier articles had been pub-lished under a variety of pen names (Khave Gross, Khane Barut, Sophie Brandt, and Clara Levin). With her flair and style, she succeeded in leav-ing the mark of her considerable writing ability and literary conscious-ness on even trivial subjects. Her articles soon came to the attention of the major Yiddish and Hebrew writers, such as Chaim Nachman Bialik,

---

5. Chava Rosenfarb, Translator's note on Lecture, University of Toronto, 1992.

Mani Leyb, and Itsik Manger. But many critics refused to believe that these articles were written by a woman. Reuven Ayzland said of her fashion section in *Der Tog* (The Day) that "it read like poetry."[6]

Anna Margolin and other Yiddish women journalists did enjoy a measure of popularity at that time. Perhaps their writing relieved the monotony of the crises and gloomy predictions that filled the newspaper headlines; more likely, they served a useful marketing function for the variety of goods and services advertised in the women's pages. In any case, although women writers found an audience, their remuneration was less than the men's, they were not given editorial responsibilities to the same degree, and their work did not appear as frequently as that of male writers. The few women who held positions of influence were often the wives and lovers of the editors, publishers, and writers. When their relationships broke up, the women frequently lost their positions at the newspapers, regardless of their journalistic and literary abilities.[7]

Margolin was dissatisfied with the major Yiddish journals for what she considered their neglect of serious poetry. In 1923, she privately published a Yiddish anthology, *The Yiddish Poem in America*. Apparently she intended to make this an annual selection, but it foundered after the first edition. The only woman included in the anthology was Celia Dropkin, who was associated with the *inzikhistn* (Introspectivists), perhaps because they shared similar concerns.

During the early decades of the twentieth century, Yiddish women writers in North America considered themselves emancipated and enlightened. They created an extensive literature that ran the gamut from chronicles of the domestic scene to the experimental and highly complex writing of Anna Margolin and others. The poet Kadya Molodowsky said of them: "They were not exotic flowers in any literary garden." They were first-generation immigrant women, part of the emerging female intelligentsia, who experienced the profound contradictions faced by most women living in North America in the twentieth century. This society held out a heady promise, yet denied them full acceptance and recognition.

Anna Margolin, a rigorous intellectual cosmopolitan in outlook, was completely dedicated to her craft. She was well-read in contemporary French, German, Hebrew, Polish, Russian, and English poetry.

---

6. Ayzland, p. 168.

7. Norma Fein Pratt, "Culture and Radical Politics: Yiddish Women Writers, 1890–1940," in *Female, Feminine and Feminist Images*, pp. 131–152.

Enamored of the work of the poet Garcia Lorca, she undertook to learn Spanish. She was greatly influenced by Baudelaire, Verlaine, and Rimbaud; among the Germans, by Else Lasker-Schüler and Rainer Maria Rilke; and among the Yiddish poets, by Itsik Manger and Avrom Sutzkever. She was knowledgeable about the major literary trends in poetry and was a formidable critic. When Margolin's collection *Lider* (Poems) was published in 1929, leading writers in Warsaw discussed her work with great admiration, and gatherings were held to read and study her poetry. Although *Lider* was well-received in New York, it did not gain the wide readership Margolin had hoped for—even though such well-known writers as Chaim Nachman Bialik and Moishe Nadir praised her work.

After the publication of *Lider,* Anna Margolin increasingly isolated herself from the company of friends and colleagues. In 1932 she ceased writing poetry altogether. Isolated in her otherness and ultimately unable to withstand the storms raging within her, she became a virtual recluse, grew obese, and suffered from depression, high blood pressure, and other ailments until her death in 1952 at the age of sixty-five.

Reuven Ayzland's description of Margolin as poet clearly sums up Margolin the person as well:

> A human being emerges out of her poetry who lives life intensely and sharply. Nothing is lukewarm to her. Everything becomes an elemental, shocking experience drawn from the broadest range of emotions: from the most refined love to the most barbarous hatred, from the deepest servility to proud admiration and contempt, from turbulent dramaticism to calm resignation, from heroic daring to almost childlike fear.[8]

According to Ayzland, Anna Margolin was so intent on safeguarding the quality of her poems that she insisted her unpublished work be destroyed upon her death. He complied with her instructions.

HER POETRY

Anna Margolin wrote at a time when most Yiddish poets belonged either to *di yunge* (The Younger Generation), or to the *inzikhistn* (The Introspectivists). *Di yunge* was a group of rebellious young poets who

---

8. Ayzland, p. 164.

sought to transcend nationalistic and political themes and were influenced by aesthetics, symbolism, and expressionism; the *inzikhistn* were interested in experimentation with form and theme and were influenced by psychoanalytic thinking. Sometimes the work of these groups was in harmony with mainstream poetic trends, sometimes not. While the male poets of her generation were discoursing and debating these trends, Anna Margolin, well-known in both circles and to some extent influenced by them, chose to remain an outsider. In spite of her relationship with Reuven Ayzland, who was the leading theoretician of *di yunge,* Anna Margolin held herself at a distance:

> I am not a child of The Younger Generation, not a grandchild nor even a (literary) comrade . . . I was not a student at their school.[9]

Anna Margolin made her poetic debut in the literary journal *Di Naye Velt* (The New World) with a poem later titled "In the Café." It appeared alongside a poem by "Albatross," which was the nom de plume of her then husband, Hirsh Leyb Gordon. Her work later appeared in various periodicals, and her collection of poetry, entitled *Lider* (Poems), appeared in New York City in 1929.

Anna Margolin organized *Lider* into six sections: Roots; I Your Calm and I Your Sword; Sealed Lips; Sun, Asphalt, Roads; Mary; and Images. The present volume also includes a supplement of later poems supplied by Abraham Novershtern that were printed in the daily newspapers after *Lider* was published.

The opening section, "Roots," beginning with the poem "Once I Was a Youth," assumes the voice of the archetypal, unrestricted male hero. The speaker depicts himself with dramatic force as a young man in pagan Greece, ancient Egypt, and Christian Rome; in this way Margolin conveys that she will not be circumscribed by the narrow, rigid confines into which women have been cast. So Margolin begins by claiming freedom in a male voice, but what is radical in her conception of gender is her sense that both masculine and feminine attributes are available to the artist, that both men and women have dual natures constantly torn between the demands of intellect and logic on the one hand and those of emotion and passion on the other. (Virginia Woolf plays with a similar theme in her novel *Orlando.*) In Margolin's poem,

---

9. S. Tenenboym, *Dikhters un doyres* (Writers and Generations) (New York, 1955), p. 166.

the speaker, traveling through the decadent ancient world, finds himself carousing in Rome, listening to "wild stories about the Jews." Compressed images and the speaker's compelling voice evoke a clash of worldviews and opposing cultures. The poem embodies an irony of history, in that the poet is a descendant of the supposedly weaker "wild" civilization while imperial Rome has long since vanished.[10] Perhaps this irony contains an oblique comment—subversive to the device of the male speaker—on the supposition that women are the "weaker sex."

In "My Ancestors Speak," Margolin presents an encapsulated history of the family, in which we can see the distancing from traditional values that the modern age exacted. In successive stanzas of this poem, Margolin reconstructs the generations of her own family and offers it up as a model for the condition of the Eastern European Jewish family after the Enlightenment. The only overtly Jewish poems Margolin wrote are to be found in this opening section of her book.

In the provocatively titled section "I Your Calm and I Your Sword," Margolin explores the themes of romantic love and failed relationships. Her poems reflect a powerful tension in the relationship between the sexes: she refuses to be lulled by a false sense of security held out by promises of love. She rejects the "feminine" voice traditionally assigned to women: coy, girlish, expressive of erotic yearnings, religious humility, sexual modesty, and sentimental motherhood. Instead, Margolin tells of disappointments, inadequacies, and conflicted yearnings. She disdains the feminine virtues of charm, delicacy, domesticity, and filial and maternal affection; instead she calls attention to the ways in which romantic love often depends on coercion and a loss of independence, freedom, and self-respect ("With Half-Closed Eyes," "You," and "Full of Night and Weeping").

Margolin's language is often theatrical in her poetic mirroring of female experience and has the mesmerizing power of incantation, as in the poem "Primeval Murderess Night":

Primeval murderess night, dark mother of necessity, help me!
Seduce him, ensnare him, swallow him, hound him to death!

Restless and observant, Anna Margolin captures the conflicts that develop when a creative woman confronts the images that male writers

---

10. Sheva Zucker, "Anna Margolin un di poezie funem geshpoltenem ikh," *YIVO Bleter*, Vol. 1 (New York, 1991), p. 177.

have imposed on her. Anna Margolin was particularly sensitive to the epithet "sentimental" and therefore strove for "hardness," tending to veil or mask her own identity in many of her poems. She frees her mind from the cold comfort of convention and breathes hard-suffering life into the truths of womanhood, giving voice to feelings of disbelief, despair, contempt, protest, and rage.

In the section called "Sealed Lips," Margolin evokes images of monsters—formless, grotesque and ominous—as in "Demons Whistled Sadly," "Demons," and "Dear Monsters." She summons up the vague threat of terror conveyed by the monsters that have recurred frequently in the female imagination. (The list starting with Mary Shelley's Frankenstein is a long one and is still being added to.) Since illusion and reality are closely intertwined, it is possible that by distorting and exaggerating reality, the writer can reveal the true nature of an experience. In spite of the horror and helplessness inspired by malevolent beings lurking behind our world, in that other realm where nightmares dwell the artist may effect a secret liberation: the artist scrutinizes the darkness, exposes ominous powers, and challenges incomprehensible forces. Harold Bloom has remarked that poetry "crosses a threshold that seems guarded by demons," and Adrienne Rich has written "a thinking woman sleeps with monsters." That Anna Margolin exemplifies these processes is clear from her work but is confirmed in a passage from a letter she wrote to Reuven Ayzland:

> I know that my devils have knives instead of teeth, and snakes instead of fingers. I can't do very much about that. I can't just get rid of them.[11]

In the section titled "Sun, Asphalt, Roads," Margolin offers up painterly images, as in the poem "Girls in Crotona Park," in which the lyric and impressionistic impetus of the poem is subverted by the girls' "bright and empty talk" and then dynamically intensified by the last line, "Botticelli loved them in his dreams." The poems about the cities she loved, "Brisk" (Brest-Litovsk) and "Odessa" illustrate her talent for lush description. Her use of repetition creates unimpeded, often exhilarating, rhythmic movement. Repetition is a central technique of the Imagists, with whom Anna Margolin is sometimes linked, although her work does not conform to many of their notions. Alliteration in "Slender Ships" creates a similar effect.

---

11. Novershtern, "Anna Margolin—Materialn tsu ir poetisher geshtalt," p. 146.

Margolin includes three poems on the subject of autumn in this section. In these poems, she overturns the conventional notions of the season as equivalent to decline and decay by conjuring up images such as "autumn shrieks," "my blood does not remember you," and "see how a naked branch flowers from the asphalt."

In the section titled "Mary," Margolin does what few Jewish writers of the time dared to do: she writes about a Christian figure, the mother of Jesus. Margolin tries to lift the burden imposed on this ordinary Jewish woman who was elevated to the status of Mother of Christ. In "What Do You Want, Mary?" Margolin attempts to reclaim Mary and to return her to her simpler, sensual beginnings:

I want my feet rooted in the earth,
to stand alone in the midst of a dew-bright field.
The sun going through me as through a young world,
the ripeness and fragrance of that dreamy field.

In "Mary Wants to Be a Beggar Woman," the speaker is Mary, but we can detect issues from Margolin's own life:

And be alone
as only kings and beggars are alone
and unhappy.
And walk thus with wondering eyes
through great, mysterious days and nights
toward the high court,
toward the painful light,
toward myself.

Margolin's Mary poems are a bold attempt to demystify Mary, to deal with her on familiar terms, woman to woman. In the way she presents the figure of Mary, Margolin conveys her own sense of uprootedness and dislocation.

The sixth and last section of Margolin's *Lider* is titled "Images." It opens with fairly conventional portraits of a madwoman and a gangster, but soon shifts to boldly include exotic imagery and erotic subject matter, including the then taboo subject of lesbianism ("On a Balcony," "My Venus Wears Silk Shoes," and "Her Smile").

In the poems in the supplementary section, Margolin casts a reflective eye on the struggles she has endured. She acknowledges that her days have been rooted in stones. Included here also is her final epitaph and the poem "Drunk from the Bitter Truth," which provides the title for the present volume. All translations with the exception of those in the supplement are based on the original volume of *Lider* published in New York in 1929. A number of poems are untitled; in these cases, they are identified by an asterisk and by their first lines.

Margolin's major themes of anxiety, loneliness, and a search for meaning run through all the sections of her book. Throughout, the great power of Margolin's poetry is that it bears a long-range memory of past customs and a sense of the layers of ancient and modern history, as in "You," but also in the "Mary" cycle, "Forgotten Gods," and "My Ancestors Speak."

Anna Margolin's central motifs include her yearning for transcendence, her resistance to the constraints of gender, and the tensions between rigid immobility and graceful movement—between proud, calm exteriors and inner turmoil, between mirror images that mock her and the masks and shawls that conceal her. These tensions spring forth when the poet's palette suddenly changes from the seeming composure of subdued hues to the brilliant colors of fire and destruction.

It becomes apparent that the overriding concerns of Anna Margolin's poetry are to undermine the established categories of the world she describes and to struggle free from social and literary confinement through redefinitions of self, art, and society, so that she can enter what Emily Dickinson called "the open space of her own authority." In that space, gentility and civility give way to primal emotion; classical calm gives way to nightmare visions of approaching specters and to the feeling that the speaker is haunted by alien yet familiar voices inimical to her well-being. Margolin's language is frequently colored by such words as the German *demerung* (twilight), an expressionist term favored by Nietzsche and Wagner and by other images that evoke apocalypse:

> For you are my conquered city ("You")

> Hair streaming in moonlight like dark rain ("My Home")

> Here, love is like a slaughter ("Her Smile")

Such images are contrasted with and shadowed by others that are diaphanous, elusive, or obscuring, as in the poem "All This Is Already Long Gone":

> Am perplexed and overcome,
> strangely touched and shaken
> by memories
> bright and pale

and like a breath of air,
so gentle.

Among Anna Margolin's strongest poems are those that offer varia-
tions on her existential dilemma and her striving for transcendence. In
the poem "In the Streets," she writes:

. . . And yet, O God, O Tormentor, I do believe
I will, even with dying fingers, touch a star
and I will hear an eternally profound,
an infinitely tender word.

Itsik Manger,[12] a Yiddish poet whom Margolin held in high re-
gard, remarked of this same poem:

Most women poets have an idyllic refuge somewhere—a home
in reality or in illusion, a grandmother, a mother, a sister, a
landscape which saves them from eternal loneliness, which
guards them from that last outcry . . . What a dramatic picture!
  But to approach (Margolin), take her by the hand, lead her
back to "granny's treasure," to mother's old-fashioned prayers,
to sister's solace, to a child's lullaby—would be a futile effort.

In the poem "Out of My Darkness," she confirms this reading:

Just as delicate wine is pressed
from trampled bloody grapes,
so have I sucked out my joy
from anguish,
and with dying hands raised it up
to the blinding savage gleam
of God's eyes.

Such poems reflect Margolin's yearning for the presence of God
in the universe and express her defiance of the impersonal, implacable
and indifferent cosmos that she is determined to penetrate. The last
lines of the poem "Beautiful Words of Marble and Gold" sum up her
defiance:

I will shrug these still beautiful shoulders,
will, perhaps, still force these trembling lips
to smile, and will succeed.

---

12. Itsik Manger, *Shriftn un proze* (Tel Aviv: Farlag I. L. Peretz, 1980), pp. 249–250.

Smiling and breathless
I exhale the weak smoke of my last cigarette
to the enormous iron mask of the heavens.

Margolin was all too aware of the implicit contradictions between her worldly pursuits, which sometimes bordered on hedonism, and her religious faith. In one of her letters she writes:

> But I haven't ever been able to be secular even though when I was very young I was a flaming anarchist. I have always talked to God, and in times of sorrow, I admit I have given God hell.[13]

Anna Margolin created her own language and style, which even now seems fresh and contemporary. Her writing is a blend of complexity and simplicity, imbued with ambiguity and dissonance; often it is an intentional construct of fragments. Her brilliance lies in the arrangement of content: as the elements of meaning find their inevitable form, juxtaposition takes on the work of statement. Often Margolin begins her poems by creating an impressionistic mood with such words as *calmly, slowly, cool, like icons*. Avraham Novershtern suggests such sensual but frozen choices imply stifled impulses.[14] In Margolin's poems, initial visions of home and belonging are soon undercut by bizarre, grotesque images of displacement and dislocation as the familiar becomes strange.

Self-examination can be dangerous, and this is the process Anna Margolin embarked on when she set out for uncharted poetic territory. In describing the creative process, Margolin wrote to Reuven Ayzland, "The creative person wears a mask . . . just like a sculptor wears an apron."[15] Yet in another letter to Ayzland, she emphasized that the artist reveals what is hidden:

---

13. Norma Fein Pratt, *Anna Margolin*. Video. Los Angeles: UCLA Educational Media Center, 1988.

14. Avraham Novershtern, "Who Would Believe That a Bronze Statue Can Weep: The Poetry of Anna Margolin," *Prooftexts: 10th Anniversary Issue* Johns Hopkins Press, 10:3, 1990, p. 445.

15. Novershtern, "Anna Margolin—Materialn tsu ir poetisher geshtalt," p. 145.

The authentic artist carries within himself another world to which the ordinary person has no access. The great value of the poet is that he enriches us with new, thoroughly experienced feelings, with unseen or differently seen landscapes.[16]

Once she had departed from the conventions of her medium for the purposes of innovation, she was no longer safe. Her concision produces complex and dense images. She was not just inventing new modes, but liberating new meanings that might well direct their forces against her. Indeed, Margolin's use of language as a means of discovery may have contributed to the illness that so completely engulfed and silenced her after the publication of her book. Wolfgang Kayser put the problem this way:

> I do not want man to be shipwrecked, but he should realize he is sailing an ocean . . . Language is dangerous . . . It can suddenly prove to be arbitrary, strange, demonically alive and capable of dragging a person into the nocturnal and inhuman sphere.[17]

If language has the ability to become energized and draw a writer into its whirlpool, depriving her of her freedom and making her afraid of the very demons she herself has invoked, it seems reasonable to speculate that Anna Margolin may have been drawn into just such a vortex, which sapped her emotional energies. Anna Margolin acknowledges her own dark nature in the poem "I Have Wandered So Much, Beloved":

> My bad blood,
> the iron rod of desire
> has chased me an entire lifetime.

In yet another poem, "Discontented," she confesses:

> Perhaps I would not be so disheartened
> if I didn't dream of poems.

---

16. Abraham Novershtern, "Anna Margolin—Materialn tsu ir poetisher geshtalt," *Yivo Bleter* New Series Band I, New York, 1991, p. 167.

17. Wolfgang Kayser, *The Grotesque in Art and Literature* (Bloomington: Indiana University Press, 1963), p. 187.

While most of the Yiddish poets of the 1920s were conventional in their use of rhyme and observed the linguistic proprieties of that time, Anna Margolin—along with other Yiddish women writers—experimented with free verse and with incongruous and jarring juxtapositions of diction and sound. Although no specific connections have been established between Anna Margolin and other Yiddish women writers, she acknowledged their general influence in a letter to Reuven Ayzland:

> If I have borrowed from anyone, it was not from men, never, only from women. And if my own work shows signs of other minds, other hearts—these are the minds and hearts of women I have encountered. I never forget them. They are always in my thoughts.[18]

Margolin's fierce, individualistic expressiveness was not at all concerned with the literary niceties. In a letter to the critic S. Tenenboym, she declared:

> My poems are not just mumblings, aromas, spiderwebs. A large part of them are texture—massive, rhythmic, broad; and the context—dramatic.[19]

In her literary correspondence with Reuven Ayzland, Anna Margolin discussed her experimentation with free verse and her refusal to be bound by traditional poetic forms:

> Why must one rhyme?. . . My work demands otherwise. I require bad rhymes because I don't want good ones . . . I know *shvayg* rhymes with *tsvayg* and *shtayg; lebn* with *shvebn* and *shtrebn; himl* with *driml* . . . but I require something different. I am insulted by the mechanical precision of the conventional rhyme. Somewhere, perhaps in only one syllable, the words should agree. I want the third and fourth lines to be subtly evocative of the first line with the colour of a word, with a sound that is but a shadow, a pale echo of the previously used sound.
> . . . .
> From this standpoint, *fleyt-zayd-toyt* is a thousand times better than *royt-noyt-broyt. Glik-tog* or *glik-umetik* is better than *plog-tog* and *glik-blik.*

---

18. Novershtern, "Who Would Believe," p. 445.
19. Tenenboym, p. 166.

. . . .

A pair of unrhythmic lines neither make a poem nor turn it into a bad poem. In the hands of a poet . . . a piece of prose is a device by which to bring out shades of colour, to strongly accent something. There are moments of poetic exaltation and even refinement that are insulted by the rhyme.[20]

Margolin was convinced of the superiority of free verse over what she considered to be a mechanical rhythm based on regular meter, which she equated with dead form. The literary climate of the 1920s in both American and European poetry was fairly receptive to a style like hers.

Though her personal life was restless and turbulent, Anna Margolin's poetic hand was bold and assured as she identified and gave voice to the powerful fissures in her life and times. Her writing focused on the conflicts resulting from her intellectual and spiritual yearnings for fulfillment as a human being, a woman, and a creative artist; as well as on the sexual tensions and the distancing from traditional Jewish values that the modern period exacted.

Anna Margolin summed up her disappointment in her achievements in a second and final epitaph, published in the newspaper *Der Tog* (The Day) in 1932 and included here in the supplement. At her request, this second epitaph, minus the first two lines, is chiseled on her gravestone.

She of the cold marble breasts
and the slender light hands,
she squandered her life
on rubbish, on nothing.

Perhaps she wanted it so, perhaps she desired
this misery, these seven knives of anguish
to spill this holy living wine
on rubbish, on nothing.

Now she lies with shattered face.
Her ravaged spirit has abandoned its cage.
Passerby, have pity, be silent—
Say nothing.

---

20. Novershtern, "Anna Margolin—Materialn tsu ir poetisher geshtalt," p. 153.

It is difficult to imagine the despair, the guilt, the isolation, and the self-contempt that prompted Anna Margolin to write these lines. Yet she cannot be labeled merely an emotionally tortured person. As W. H. Auden advised: "Read the work, forget the life." However much Margolin's difficulties overwhelmed her daily life, in the realm of poetry she showed true genius and the strength to preserve her unique vision. She valued stringent honesty however exacting and painful its demands. In one of her last poems, titled "Drunk from the Bitter Truth," she states her artistic credo:

> Drunk from the bitter truth
> I refuse all other wine.

Although Anna Margolin was neglected by male critics of her time, who dismissed her as a "woman writer," and her reputation suffered during the general decline of interest in Yiddish writing, now after more than half a century of obscurity, her work has been rediscovered. A new generation of feminist scholars—Adrienne Cooper, Marcia Falk, Kathryn Hellerstein, Norma Fein Pratt, Sheva Zucker, and others—are reappraising Margolin's achievement. Her poetry, reissued in a Yiddish edition,[21] speaks to us across the generations with perhaps even greater strength today than it had in her lifetime. Anna Margolin dreamed of immortality. In the last of her three poems titled "Autumn," she wrote:

> Heavy autumn, heavy step, I am old.
> Dark heart of mine, don't curse, believe in miracles:
> somewhere in the world, in a city
> I am flowering like a lily.

May her vision be fulfilled.

---

21. Anna Margolin, *Poems* (Jerusalem: Magnes Press, Hebrew University, 1991).

Photograph of Anna Margolin's gravestone, Brooklyn, New York

a note on the translation

Translation is important for the work of most writers but is now espe-
cially so for Yiddish writers, whose situation is tragic because of the utter
break in continuity caused by the Shoah. Before World War II, a vibrant
Yiddish culture flourished in Eastern Europe in such cities as Warsaw,
Vilna, Odessa, Lemberg, and Bialystok. Everything that was connected
with that Yiddish world—art, literature, music, cafés, cinemas, educa-
tional and research centers, houses of worship and of study, newspapers,
political parties, theaters, together with several generations of artists and
writers and the millions of people who lived, spoke, and read Yiddish and
supported this culture—was destroyed in the Shoah.

In that vanished setting, Anna Margolin's ancestors—and my
own—had taken root, creating a world that pulsated to its own inner
rhythms, which evolved over many generations. Suddenly it was annihi-
lated; only a remnant survived. Translators of most languages have access
to speakers and readers of the source language and can turn to writers in
that language for clarification of difficult aspects of a text. As a translator
of Yiddish, I often find myself confronting the void created by the loss
of millions of Yiddish-speaking Jews. It was therefore with a sense of
urgency as well as obligation that I undertook to make the treasure of
Anna Margolin's poetry available in English.

I came to the poetry of Anna Margolin as a member of the Yid-
dish Women Writers' Study Group in Toronto. We began by reading
poetry in Yiddish, and Anna Margolin's poems made an immediate
powerful impression on me: her images possessed me like a *dybbuk*. Mar-
golin haunted me for the better part of five years as I tried to understand
her work. As I wrote draft translations, I often felt that she was speaking
through me and sometimes even for me. During this process, when the
meaning of a particularly troubling phrase or image suddenly revealed it-
self to me, I would experience a sense of "joyous rapture." Rilke used this
term to describe the heightened state he found himself in when translat-
ing the poetry of Paul Valéry. As a descendant of a Hassidic family, I am

familiar with this state. I know it as התלהבות—*hislayves* in Yiddish or, as it is pronounced in Hebrew, *hitlahavut*.

Anna Margolin carefully molded her poems until they were as close to perfection as she could make them. A translator of her work confronts several features that impose conflicting demands on the translation: spareness and exoticism, ambiguity and precision, explicit language and implicit feeling. All these features are evident in the poem "Portrait," from the first section of the book, called "Roots":

> Because mockery and sorrow inflamed her life,
> she held her head proudly
> as if God had secretly elated her.
>
> In the empty house, peering into the mirror as through rain,
> as if familiar eyes were watching her,
> she approached herself solemnly,
> as one approaches an Infanta.
>
> Calmly, calmly, sitting stiff and formal.
> Not even entrusting her mask to the solitude
> when the pleasant evening hours
> hover mournfully over her and over all.
> Feeling only bleak, burning madness
> tighten gently round her throat.

I have paid meticulous attention to the meanings of particular words and have constantly weighed the choice between being faithful to literal meanings and being faithful to structure, diction, and style. As in all poetry of high caliber, the two sets of elements are so strongly bonded in Margolin's poetry as to be virtually inseparable. There is a Yiddish folk saying that sums up this dilemma: "He who translates literally is a liar, and he who alters a text is a blasphemer and a libeler." Throughout, Ezra Pound's advice, "Let Homer speak," and Borges's challenging demand, "Don't translate what I say, but what I wanted to say," rang in my ears as I tried to divine the intent of Margolin's words.

In rendering both the sense of the poems and their distinctive voice, I have sometimes had to abandon (however reluctantly) any attempt to reproduce their metrical structure and rhyme schemes. I was willing to do this as long as I could retain the spirit, tone, and meaning of the poem. My goal has been to create as nearly as possible in English an effect similar to the one Margolin's poems produce in Yiddish. But Yiddish diction and sentence patterns are often difficult to capture in English, as in the closing eight lines of the poem "Odessa":

אָון קענט איר זיך דערמאָנען;
אַלץ דאָס, וואָס האָט ניט קיין נאָמען
און איז בלויז אַ דופֿט און אַ סוד?
און דעם אָטעם פֿון סטעפּ,
און פֿון זון, און פֿון סמאָלע?
און צום זינגענדן ים האָט די שטאָט,
ווי מיט אַ זײַדענעם שלעפּ,
געניׄדערט פֿון טויזנט מירמעלנע טרעפּ.

Un kent ir zikh dermonen
alts dos, vos hot nit keyn nomen
un iz bloyz a duft un a sod?
un dem otem fun step,
un fun zun, un fun smole?
un tsum zingendn yam hot di shtot,
vi mit a zaydenem shlep,
genidert fun toyznt mirmelne trep.

A literal translation would render this as follows:

And can you remember
all that which has no name
and is only a scent and a secret?
and the breath of the steppe,
and the sun and the tar?
and to the singing sea did the city,
as with a silken pull,
let down from a thousand marble steps.

The first five lines in translation can be fairly straightforward regarding syntax, although "mystery" is an important adjustment since the closing "sea" rhymes with it, but the last three lines required changes to both syntax and line units:

And can you remember
everything that has no name
is only a fragrance, a mystery?
and a breath of the steppe,
of sun and of tar?
The city lowered,
as if by a silken cord,
down a thousand marble steps
into the singing sea.

For instance, the Yiddish text rhymes "dermonen / nomen," "sod / shtot," and "step / shlep / trep." In my translation, I have tried at least to echo some of this rhyming. Alliterative patterns create a texture of sound in "remember / no name," "lowered / cord," and "city / silken / steps / singing sea," and the chain of syllables "remem_ber / tar_ / low_ ered." I chose to alter the syntax of the last three lines of the Yiddish, both to avoid subject-verb inversion (which sounds stilted or archaic in English) and to end on "sea." And I changed the line units to produce a cadenced movement and to avoid ending up with one line that would have been longer than any of Margolin's in this passage.

One common view of translation is that it should simultaneously be true to the source text and read as if it were written in the target language. In this view, the translation should not call attention to itself, or the translator will come between the writer and the reader. But that is where the translator inevitably is, as Walter Benjamin famously pointed out in "The Task of Translation,"[1] and although achieving a convincing naturalness in the target language is a worthwhile aspiration, it is also the case that if translations never stretched established usage in the target language, they would never expand the resources and the repertoire of that language and its literature. I am grateful to Roger Greenwald for our discussions of these issues. So I don't believe in reducing subtleties in order to make a work more accessible in translation than it is to begin with, even as I aspire to make poems that work in English. I can only hope that my translations succeed well enough to give readers access to an important and highly individualistic writer whose passion and intelligence combine in memorable poetry.

---

1. Lawrence Venuti, ed. *Translation Studies Reader* (London: Routledge), 2000.

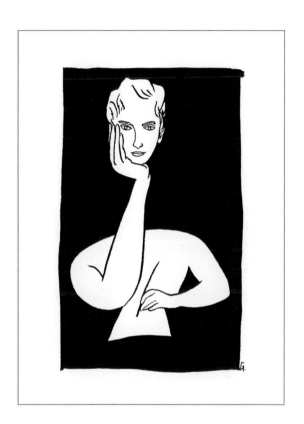

Anna Margolin

Poems

ROOTS

וואָרצלען

Vortslen

איך בין געווען אַ מאָל אַ ייִנגלינג

איך בין געווען אַ מאָל אַ ייִנגלינג
געהערט אין פּאַרטיקאַס סאַקראַטן
עס האָט מײַן בוזעם-פֿרײַנד, מײַן ליבלינג,
געהאַט דעם שענסטן טאָרס אין אַטען.

געוועזן צעזאַר. און אַ העלע וועלט
געבויט פֿון מאַרמאָר, איך דער לעצטער,
און פֿאַר אַ ווײַב מיר אויסדערוויילט
מײַן שטאָלצע שוועסטער.

אין רויזנקראַנץ בײַם ים ווײַן ביז שפּעט
געהערט אין הויכמוטיקן פֿרידן
וועגן שוואָקלינג פֿון נאַזאַרעט
און ווילדע מעשׂיות וועגן ייִדן.

2

ONCE I WAS A YOUTH

Once I was a youth,
heard Socrates in the porticoes,
my bosom friend, my lover,
in all Athens had the finest torso.

I was Caesar. And a bright world
built of marble. I the last
chose for a bride
My proud sister.

Garlanded and drunk till late
in boisterous revelry, I heard the news
of the weakling from Nazareth
and wild stories about the Jews.

מוטער ערד, פֿיל געטראָטענע, זון-געוואַשענע

מוטער ערד, פֿיל געטראָטענע, זון-געוואַשענע,

טונקעלע שקלאַפֿין און האַרין

בין איך, געליבטער.

פֿון מיר דער ניד'ריקער און דער באַטריבטער

וואַקסטו אַרויס — אַ מעכטיקער שטאַם.

און ווי די אייביקע שטערן, און ווי פֿון זון דער פֿלאַם,

קריִז איך אין לאַנגן און בלינדן שוויַיגן

אין דיַינע וואָרצלען, אין דיַינע צוויַיגן,

און האַלב אין וואַך, און האַלב אין דרימל

זוך איך דורך דיר דעם הויכן הימל.

4

MOTHER EARTH, WELL-WORN, SUN-WASHED

Mother earth, well-worn, sun-washed,

dusky slave and mistress

am I, beloved.

From me, humble and dejected

you arise—a mighty trunk.

Like the eternal stars, like the sun's flame,

I circle in long blind silence round

your roots, your boughs.

Half awake and half drowsing,

I search through you for heaven on high.

פּאָרטרעט

א. לעיעלעס'ן

ווייל שפּאַט און אומגליק האָבן דורכגעגליט איר לעבן,
האָט זי געטראָגן אַזוי שטאָלץ דעם קאָפּ,
ווי ס'וואָלט זי גאָט געהיימנישפֿול דערהויבן.

אין לערן הויז, אין שפּיגל זיך געזען ווי דורך אַ רעגן,
און ווי עס וואָלטן אַלץ איר נאָכגעקוקט באַקאַנטע,
איז זי פֿייערלאָך געגאַנגען זיך אַנטקעגן,
ווי מען גייט אַנטקעגן אַן אינפֿאַנטע.

געראָט, געראָט. געזעסן גלײַך און שטײַף.
און ניט פֿאַרטרויט איר מאַסקע אויף דער איינזאַמקייט,
ווען ס'האָבן גוטע אָוונטיקע שעהען
יאָמערנדיק געניגט זיך איבער איר און איבער אַלץ.
און נאָר געפֿילט: וויסטער, פֿלאָמיקער שגעון
דריקט צערטלעך איר צונויף דעם האַלדז.

6

PORTRAIT

* To A. Leyeles

Because mockery and sorrow inflamed her life,

she held her head proudly

as if God had secretly elated her,

In the empty house, peering into the mirror as through rain,

as if familar eyes were watching her,

she approached herself solemnly,

as one approaches an Infanta.

Calmly, calmly, sitting stiff and formal.

Not even entrusting her mask to the solitude,

when the pleasant evening hours

hover mournfully over her and over all.

Feeling only bleak, burning madness

tighten gently round her throat.

*Aaron Glanz-Leyeles (1889–1966)
Founder of *In-zikh* movement.

יאָרן

ווי פֿרויען, וועלכע זײַנען פֿיל גיליבט און דאָך ניט זאַט,
און גייען דורכן לעבן מיט געלעכטער און מיט צאָרן
אין די אויגן זייערע פֿון פֿײַער און אגאַט —
געווען אַזוי זײַנען די יאָרן.

און זײַנען אויך געוועזן ווי אַקטיאָרן,
וואָס שפּילן מיט אַ האַלב מויל "האַמלעט" פֿאַרן מאַרק;
ווי אין לאַנד, אַ שטאָלצן, גראַנסיניאָרן,
וואָס כאַפֿן אָן דעם אויפֿשטאַנד פֿאַרן קאַרק.

און זע, ווי דעמוטיק זיי זײַנען איצט, מײַן גאָט,
און שטום ווי אַ צעשמעטערטער קלאַוויר,
און נעמען אָן פֿאַר ליב אײַעדנס שטויס און שפֿאַט,
און זוכן דיך, ניט גלויבנדיק אין דיר.

8

YEARS

Like women well loved yet still not sated,
going through life with laughter and rage
eyes gleaming with fire and agate—
that's how the years were.

They were also like actors, insipidly
playing Hamlet in the square,
like grand seigneurs in a proud land
who grab rebellion by the throat.

See how submissive they are now, my God,
struck dumb as a shattered piano,
taking each blow and taunt like a caress,
seeking You, yet not believing in You.

אין גאַסן

דאָ אַ וואָרט מיט שרעק און דאָ פֿול מיט חרטה.

דאָ האָב איך געוויינט און דאָ אין צער גערוט.

האָסט אַלע גאַסן דאָך פֿאַרוואַנדלט אין גאָלגאָטע.

אין אַלע גאַסן רינט מײַן בלוט.

דאָ האָב איך געוויינט. עס האָבן דומפֿ די מויערן

געברומט דעם גזר-הדין אויף שוואַכע און פֿאַרלוירערענע.

און ס'האָבן נאָכגעקוקט פֿיל דאַמען און פֿיל הערן,

ווי ס'גייט אַ פֿרוי דורך דעמערונג אין טרערן.

געווען געבעט, און צאָרן געווען, חרטה.

און איצט שרײַט אויף די לעצטע שרעקן-פֿולע נאָטע

פֿון לעבן, זינקענדיק אין שטויב.

און דאָך, אַ גאָט, אַ פֿײַניקער, איך גלויב:

איך וועל מיט פֿינגער גוססע נאָך אָנרירן אַ שטערן

און אַן אומענדלעך טיף, אומענדלעך צערטלעך וואָרט דערהערן.

10

IN THE STREETS

Here a word of terror, there one of regret.

Here I cried out, there in sorrow I paused.

You transformed the roads into Golgotha,

and my blood runs in all the streets.

Here I wept. The dank walls

roared out the stern judgment at the weak and the lost

while many lords and ladies looked on

as the woman walked through the dusk in tears.

Pleading, raging, regretting,

now the last terrible note of life

blares forth, sinking into the dust.

And yet, O God, O Tormentor, I do believe:

With dying fingers, I will yet touch a star,

and I will hear an eternally profound,

an infinitely tender word.

מיַין שטאַם רעדט

מיַין שטאַם:

מענער אין אַטלעס און סאַמעט,

פּנימער לאַנג און בלייכזיַדן,

פֿאַרחלש'טע גלוטיקע ליפן.

די דינע הענט צערטלען פֿאַרגעלטע פֿאָליאַנטן.

זיי רעדן אין טיפֿער נאַכט מיט גאָט.

און סוחרים פֿון ליַיפּסק און פֿון דאַנסק.

בלאַנקע מאַנקעטן. איידעלער סיגאַרן-רויך.

גמרא-וויצן. דיַיטשע העפֿלעכקייטן.

דער בליק איז קלוג און מאַט,

קלוג און איבערזאַט.

דאָן-זשואַנען, העַנדלער און זוכער פֿון גאָט.

אַ שיכּור,

אַ פּאָר משומדים אין קיעוו.

מיַין שטאַם:

פֿרויען ווי געצן באַצירט מיט בריליאַנטן,

פֿאַרטונקלט רויט פֿון טערקישע טיכער,

שווערע פֿאַלדן פֿון סאַטין-דע-ליאָן.

אָבער דאָס ליַיב איז אַ וויינענדיקע ווערבע,

אָבער ווי טרוקענע בלומען די פֿינגער אין שויס,

12

My ancestors:

Men in satin and velvet,

faces long and silky pale,

faintly glowing lips

and thin hands caressing faded folios.

Deep into the night they speak with God.

Merchants from Leipzig and Danzig

with clean cuffs, smoking fine cigars.

Talmudic wit. German niceties.

Their look is clever and lacklustre,

clever and self-satisfied.

Don Juans, dealers and seekers of God.

A drunkard,

a pair of converts in Kiev.

My ancestors:

Women bejewelled in diamonds like icons,

darkly crimsoned by Turkish shawls,

and heavy folds of Satin-de-Lyon.

But their bodies are weeping willows,

the fingers in their laps like withered flowers,

און אין די וועלקע פֿארשלייערטע אויגן
טויטע לוסט.

און גראַנד-דאַמען אין ציץ און אין ליַװונט,
נרייַטבייניק און שטאַרק, און באַװעגלעך,
מיטן פֿאַראַכטלעכן לײַכטן געלעכטער,
מיט רוויִקע רייד און אומהיימלעכן שװײַגן.
פֿאַר נאַכט בײַם פֿענצטער פֿון אָרעמען הויז
װאַקסן זיי װי סטאַטוען אויס
און עס צוקט דורך די דעמערענדע אויגן
גרויזאַמע לוסט.

און אַ פֿאָר,
מיט װעלכע איך שעם זיך.

זיי אַלע, מײַן שטאַם,
בלוט פֿון מײַן בלוט
און פֿלאַם פֿון מײַן פֿלאַם,
טויט און לעבעדיק אויסגעמישט,
טרויעריק, גראָטעסק און גרויס
טראַמפּלען דורך מיר װי דורך אַ טונקל הויז.
טראַמפּלען מיט תּפֿילות און קללות און קלאָג,
טרייסלען מײַן האַרץ װי אַ קופּערנעם גלאָק,
עס װאַרפֿט זיך מײַן צונג,
איך דערקען ניט מײַן קול —
מײַן שטאַם רעדט.

14

and in their faded, veiled eyes

lifeless desire.

Grand ladies in calico and linen,

broad-boned, strong and agile,

with their contemptuous, easy laughter,

with calm talk and uneasy silence.

At dusk, by the window of the humble house

they sprout like statues.

And coursing through their dusky eyes

cruel desire.

And a pair

I am ashamed of.

All of them, my ancestors,

blood of my blood,

flame of my flame,

dead and living mixed together,

sad, grotesque, immense.

They trample through me as through a dark house.

Trampling with prayers, and curses, and wailing,

rattling my heart like a copper bell,

my tongue quivers,

I don't know my own voice—

My ancestors speak.

ווען איז עס געווען? איך קען זיך ניט דערמאָנען.

עס גייט מיר נאָך ווי אַ פֿאַרגעסענער רעפֿרען:

אַ שטאָט ביים ים, נאָקטיורנען פֿון שאָפּען

און איזיאָרנע ליליען פֿון באַלקאַנען.

פֿאַר נאַכט. צוויי שוועסטער מיט די שמאָלע פֿינגער

פֿאַרטרוימטע רירן אָן דעם שאַטנדיקן שטראָם

פֿון זכרונות אין אַלטמאָדישן אַלבאָם.

די אַלטע בילדער ווערן לאַנגזאָם ייִנגער.

אין טיר האַלב אָפֿענער, דאָרט צווישן די וואַזאָנען,

פֿאַרחלשט שווימען פּאָרלעך אין אַ לאשטשענדיקן וואַלס.

אַ, טויטע יוגנט! אַ, דער לעצטער וואַלס!

די טענצער שווימען און פֿאַרשווינדן ווי פֿאַנטאָמען...

עס איז געווען, געווען... איך קען זיך ניט דערמאָנען.

16

A CITY BY THE SEA

When was it? I can't remember.
It follows me like a forgotten refrain:
A city by the sea, Chopin's nocturnes
and cast-iron lilies on the balconies.

Dusk. Two sisters, their slender fingers
dreamily fondle the shadowy stream
of memories in an old-fashioned album.
Slowly, the old photographs grow younger.

Through the half-open door, among potted plants,
trancelike couples in a caressing waltz.
Oh, dead youth! Oh, last waltz!
The dancers waft by and vanish like phantoms. . . . .

It was . . . was . . . I can't remember.

הײַזער וויגן זיך און שווימען ליכטיק-גרוי

מיט פֿײַכטע גערטנער, זילבער-העלע גאַסן,

און מענטשן בײַ שוועלן פֿון טירן

נייגן זיך, שמייכלען, פֿאַרבלאַסן,

ווערן און ניט ווערן

דורכן רעגן-בויגן פֿון טרערן.

אַ קינד זיצט בײַם פֿענצטער.

אין לבֿנה-שײַן שטראָמען די האָר ווי טונקעלער רעגן.

פֿאַרעקשנ'ט און ליכטיק זוכן די אויגן

ווי דורך אַ וואַלד

די אייגענע וויַיטע געשטאַלט.

אָ, וואָס ציטערסטו, קינד,

ווען איך קום דיר אַנטקעגן?

MY HOME

Houses sway and float in the light gray

of damp gardens, clear silvery streets,

and people in doorways

bow, smile, fade,

appear and disappear

through a rainbow of tears.

A child sits by the window,

hair streaming in the moonlight like dark rain,

eyes stubbornly and brightly seek

its own distant form

as through a forest.

Oh, why do you tremble, child,

when I draw near?

I YOUR CALM AND

I YOUR SWORD

איך דײַן רו און

איך דײַן שווערד

Ikh dayn ru un

ikh dayn shvert

מיר זײַנען געגאַנגען דורך טעג ווי דורך שטורעם-דורכציטערטע גערטנער.

געבליט און גערײַפֿט און געאיבט זיך אין שפּילן מיט לעבן און טויט.

כמאַרע און ברייטקייט און טראָים איז געוועזן אין אונדזערע ווערטער.

און צווישן פֿאַרעקשנטע ביימער אין זומערדיק-רוישנדע גערטנער

האָבן מיר זיך פֿאַרצווײַגט אין איין אייציקן בוים.

און אָוונטן האָבן געשפּרייט זיך מיט שווערע פֿאַרטונקלטער בלוייקייט,

מיטן שמערצלעכן גלוסטן פֿון ווינטן און פֿאַלנדע שטערן,

מיטן בלאָנדזשענדן לאַשטשענדן שׂין איבער צוקנדע גראָזן און בלעטער,

און מיר האָבן פֿאַרוועבט זיך אין ווינט, אײַנגעזאַפֿט זיך אין בלוייקייט

און געוווען ווי די גליקלעכע חיות און ווי קלוגע און שפּילנדע געטער.

22

We went through the days as through storm-tossed gardens.
Blossoming, maturing; mastering the game of life and death.
Clouds, vastness and dreams were in our words.
Among stubborn trees in a rustling summer garden
we fused into a single tree.

Evenings spread their deeply darkened blue,
with the aching desire of winds and falling stars,
with shifting, caressing glow of fluttering leaves and grasses,
we wove ourselves into the wind, merged with the blueness
like happy creatures and clever, playful gods.

מיט האַלב פֿאַרמאַכטע אויגן

זיצנדיק בײַם טיש אין גרויען זאַל,
פֿויל און אומרויִק זיך וויקלענדיק אין שאַל,
קוק איך דען אויף דיר?
רוף דיך דען צו מיר?
נאָר רויטער איז מײַן מויל אַצינד,
און די האַלב פֿאַרמאַכטע אויגן
מיט אַ רויך פֿאַרצויגן.

נאָר פֿאַרפֿלייצט בין איך פֿון רויש און ליכט,
און דײַן געזיכט זע איך דורך נעפל און פֿלאַם,
און אויף די ליפֿן איז שאַרף דער טעם
פֿון זון און וואינט.

נאָר איך צי זיך אַרויף מיט פֿאַרשטיקטן געשריי,
איך וואַקס פֿלאַטערנדיק, פֿיבערדיק אַזוי,
און דאָס וואַקסן טוט ווייי.

פֿאַררוקט אין ווינקל פֿון דעם גרויען זאַל,
אין די לאַנגע פֿלאַמענדיקע פֿאַלדן פֿון שאַל,
קוק איך דען אויף דיר?
רוף דיך דען צו מיר?
נאָר איך האָב ווייטאָגלעך, און טיף, און בלינד
מיט האַלב פֿאַרמאַכטע אויגן
דיך אײַנגעזויגן.

24

WITH HALF-CLOSED EYES

Sitting at the table in the gray hall,

lazy and restless, wrapped in my shawl,

am I looking at you?

Am I calling you?

My mouth is redder now,

my half-closed eyes

are veiled in smoke.

I am flooded with noise and light,

I see your face through fog and flame,

on my lips is the sharp taste

of sun and wind.

I pull myself up with stifled roar,

I grow frenzied, shivering

and this growth is pain.

Huddled in a corner of the gray hall,

in the long, flaming folds of my shawl,

am I looking at you?

Am I calling you?

Yet, painfully, deeply, blindly

with half-closed eyes, I have

drawn you in.

לאַנגזאַם און ליכטיק

לאַנגזאַם און ליכטיק

האָסטו דײַן שװערן שטערן צוגעבויגן צו מײַן שטערן,

ביסטו פֿאַרזונקען מיט דײַן שװאַרצן פֿײַער

אין מײַן בלױען פֿײַער.

און מײַן צימער איז געװאָרן פֿול מיט זומער,

און מײַן צימער איז געװאָרן פֿול מיט נאַכט.

האָב איך מײַנע לױכטנדיקע װײַנענדיקע אױגן צוגעמאַכט,

האָב איך געװײנט שטיל אין מײַן שפּעטן זומער.

26

SLOWLY AND BRIGHTLY

Slowly and brightly
you bent your heavy brow to mine,
and your black fire
sank into my blue fire.

My room was filled with summer,
my room was filled with night.
I closed my shining, weeping eyes,
and wept quietly in my late summer.

האָב אַזוי פֿיל געוואַנדערט, מײַן ליבער,

דורך פֿרעמדע און טונקעלע לעבנס,

דורך הערצער ווי חרובֿע לענדער —

זײ גוט.

האָב געוווּסט טויזנט טויטן, מײַן ליבער.

און צום לעבן געיאָגט יעדעס מאָל

האָט בײַז בלוט,

פֿון לוסט די אײַזערנע רוט.

מענטש מיטן שטילן קול,

מענטש פֿון סאַמעט און שטאָל,

בײג זיך טיף איבער מיר,

פֿאַרשטעל די וועלט פֿון מיר

און אויך מײַן אייגן בלוט.

זײ גוט.

"I HAVE WANDERED SO MUCH"

I have wandered so much, beloved,

through strange and dark lives,

through hearts like wastelands—

be kind.

Known a thousand deaths, beloved.

My bad blood,

the iron rod of desire,

has chased me an entire lifetime.

Man of velvet and of steel,

man, with quiet voice,

hover over me,

shield me from the world

and from my own blood also.

Be kind.

איך גיי דורך דיר אין באַרבאַרישן גלאַנץ, ווי דררך אַ באַזיגטער שטאַט.

פֿיר נעגערלעך טראָגן די עק פֿון מײַן גאָלד-געשטיקן, מיט פֿאַוועס און מאָנבלומען אויסגענייטן מאַנטל. הינטער מיר גייען קריגסלײַט, בלינדיק מיט די קורצע שווערדן, נאַקעטע אָרעמס און קני; פֿריסטער אין ווײַסן לײַוונט; אַ גאַנצע שאַר פֿאַזן אין שוואַרצן זײַד און פֿורפור; און עס שטאַמפֿן ברייטע העלפֿאַנדן און טראָגן אויף זייערע רוקנס די פֿריידיקע געטער פֿון מײַן היימלאַנד, די הייליקע מאַלפעס און פֿאַרביקע פֿייגל, וואָס שרײַען אויף זיס און ווילד אונטערן פֿרעמדן הימל.

איך גיי דורך דיר, ווי דורך אַ באַזיגטער שטאַט.

יובלענדע שטימען וואַרפֿן ווי אַ פֿאַרצערנדן פֿלאַם מײַן נאָמען צום הימל, און צוריק פֿאַלט ער צעשפֿליטערט אין טאַנצנדע פֿונקען. אין הויפֿנס ליגן שמאַראַגדן, עמעראַלדן, רובינען, וועלכע דו האָסט אויסגעגראָבן פֿון דײַן טיפֿעניש, אַלע נאָך אַרומגעקלעפּט מיט דײַן ערד, און בלוט, און צער.

אָבער אַ, יענע טונקעלע און געדרייטע גאַסן, וועלכע איך האָב מורא צו באַטרעטן. יענע וואַכעדיקע שטילקייט אין דיר, אין וועלכער מײַן נאָמען האָט מאָל קיין ניט געזונגען... און שאָטנס, וואָס בײַגן זיך פֿאַר מיר ניט...

און ביסט מײַן באַזיגטע שטאַט. אין דײַנע אומעטיקע ווי סטע טעמפּלען האָב איך אַוועקגעשטעלט מײַנע געטער. און דאָס ליד, וואָס דו פֿרווווסט פֿאַר זיי זינגען מיט אַן אומזיכער קול, איז ווי זון און ליבע.

30

YOU

I pass through you in barbarous splendour, as through a conquered city.
Four little pygmies carry my train, gold embroidered with peacocks and poppies.
Behind me march the warriors flashing their short swords, arms and knees bare.
Priests in white linen, an entire troop of poets in black and purple silk; and broad,
stomping elephants carrying on their backs the joyous gods of my native land,
the holy monkeys and the colorful birds that shrill sweet and wild under alien
skies.

I pass through you as through a conquered city.

My name is hurled heavenward like a raging flame by jubilant voices only to fall
back and crack into dancing sparks. Your jewels lie in heaps, emeralds and rubies
you dug out of your depths—your own earth—your blood and your sorrow still
clinging to them.

But, oh, those gloomy, crooked streets on which I fear to tread. That watchful
stillness in you, in which my name never sang . . . and shadows that do not bend
toward me. . .

For you are my conquered city. In your sad and empty temples I placed my gods.
And that song you tried to sing to them in uncertain voice is like sunshine and
love.

31

אָבער יענע שטילע און איינזאַמע ווינקלען. איך האָב אין דער פֿינצטערניש געזען

שפֿאַטנדיקע אויגן. איך האָב געזען דעם בליאַסק פֿון אַ מעסער. און ווען דו האָסט ווי

מיט טויזנט הענט מיך אַרומגענומען אין דער נאַכט, איז אין אַלע טויזנט הענט געווען

צעשטערונג,

But in those silent, lonely corners I saw mocking eyes through the darkness. I saw the glint of a knife. When you embraced me as with a thousand hands in the night, in all those thousand hands was destruction.

דרימל אײַן, געליבטער, דרימל.
ביסט ווי יונגע ברוינע וואַלדערד.
דײַנע אויגן זײַנען פֿול מיט הימל.

איך דײַן רו און איך דײַן שווערד
וואַך איצט איבער ערד און הימל.
יעדער שטערן שטוינט און הערט,
וואָס איך פֿליסטער אין דײַן דרימל.

34

"DROWSE ON, MY BELOVED"

Drowse on, my beloved, drowse on.
You are like new brown forest earth.
Your eyes are full of sky.

I your peace and I your sword
now watch over heaven and earth.
Every star in amazement hears
what I whisper in your sleep.

וויאָלינען

דער בלוויער טרוים פֿון וויאָלינען.

איך און דו,

אַזעלכע ווײַזע,

אַזעלכע ווײַזע,

און ס'ווייס ניט קיינער,

אַז מיר קרײַזן

אין גאָלדענע רינגען,

ווי שמעטערלינגען,

אין דער בלוויער נאַכט פֿון וויאָלינען.

דו מײַן רו,

אונדזער נאַכט,

און מיך, און דיך

שפּילן די בלויע וויאָלינען.

36

VIOLINS

The blue dream of violins.

I and you,

such a revelation,

such a revelation,

and nobody knows,

that we circle

in golden rings

like butterflies,

in the blue night of violins.

You, my peace,

our night,

the blue violins play

for me and for you.

אין קופּער און אין גאָלד

אין קופּער און אין גאָלד פֿון די מטבעות
לײַכט קיל און קלאָר דאָס פּנים פֿון אַ קעניג,
און ס'ליגט די וועלט בײַ אונדזער שוועל, פֿאַרכּישופֿט
פֿון ווײַטן אָפּשײַן פֿון דעם קעניג.

אויף אַלע העלע און אויף טונקעלע זאַכן
איז אויסגעקריצט דאָס פּנים פֿון מײַן קעניג.
און ס'זינגען גאָלדן-שווער איצט אַלע זאַכן,
און גאָלדן בליט די וועלט בײַ מיר אין האַרצן,
פֿאַרכּישופֿט פֿון דײַן ווײַטן שײַן, מײַן קעניג.

38

IN COPPER AND IN GOLD

The king's face glows cool and clear
from copper and gold coins.
The world lies spellbound at our doorstep
by this distant reflection of the king.

The face of my king is etched
on all things bright and dark.
Everything is now laden with gold.
The world flowers golden within me,
enchanted by your distant gleam, my king.

עס רעדן הײַנט אַלע שטומע זאַכן.

עס רינט ווי טוי

דאָס בלויע פֿליסטערן פֿון שלאַנקן וואַלקן.

הויכע קלוגע ווערטער רוישן אין די קרוינען פֿון די ביימער,

פֿון די אַלטע, געוואַלדיקע טרויימער,

און פֿאַלן אין מײַן האַרץ מיט יעדן בלאַט און יעדן שטערן.

און קענסטו הערן,

ווי עס ציטערט דער זאַמד

אונטער די אײַנזאַמע לאַנגזאַמע טריט פֿון דער נאַכט?

און פֿײַערלעך און גרויס

קײַקלט זיך אַרויס

אַ ברייט געזאַנג

פֿון דעם גרויען, מיט שאָטנס אומרינגלטן שטיין.

און דו, מײַן ליבער, מײַן ליבער,

דו שווײַגסט.

"ALL MUTE THINGS SPEAK TODAY"

All mute things speak today.

The blue murmuring of a whispy cloud

falls like dew.

Lofty words from the great dreamers of old

rustle in the treetops

and fall on my heart with every leaf and every star.

Can you hear it—

how the sand is quivering

under the lonely, slow tread of night?

Solemnly and grandly

a rich chant

peals forth

from the gray, shrouded stone.

And you, my dear, my dear,

you are silent.

מיט באַנגע העמנט האַלט איך דײַן ליבן קאָפּ,

און שװער און טונקל פֿון די גרױסע אױגן

שטײגט דײַן פֿאַרשאָטנט לעבן מיר אַנטקעגן.

אַ שטילע שרעק בײגט מיך צו דיר אַראָפּ ––

זאָל גאָט דיך היטן.

האָבן מיר דען ניט גענוג געליטן?

װאָס מאָנט דער שאָטן צװישן האָרכנדיקע צװײַגן?

װאָס בעט די טיפֿע טרױעריקע שטימע אין דעם שװײַגן?

דורך טרערן בײַג איך זיך צו דיר אַראָפּ

און טרינק דאָס טונקלע לעבן דײַנס מיט באַנגע ליפּן.

42

"WITH ANXIOUS HANDS"

With anxious hands I hold your precious head,

the large eyes heavy and dark

raise up your shadowed life toward me.

A quiet terror bows me down to you—

May God watch over you.

Have we not suffered enough?

What does that shadow among the listening branches demand?

What does that deep mournful voice in the silence ask?

Through my tears I bow down to you

and drink your dark life with uneasy lips.

פֿול מיט נאַכט און געוויין

אַ שוויַיגן פלוצעם און טיף
צווישן אונדז ביַידן,
ווי אַ צעטומלטער בריוו
מיטן אָנזאָג פון שיַידן.
ווי אַ זינקענדע שיף.

אַ שוויַיגן אָן אַ בליק, אָן אַ ריר,
פֿול מיט נאַכט און געוויין
צווישן אונדז ביַידן,
ווי מיר וואָלטן אַליַין
צו אַ גן-עדן
פֿאַרשליסן די טיר.

44

FULL OF NIGHT AND WEEPING

A silence, sudden and deep

between us,

like a bewildering letter

that announces a parting.

Like a ship going down.

A silence, without a glance, without a stir,

full of night and weeping

between us,

as if we ourselves

had bolted the door

to a Garden of Eden.

דערהערט דײַנע טריט און זיך דערשראָקן —
איך האָב מײן קול ניט דערקענט.

אָ, טײַערער און באַגערטער,
אין אומגעהױערן צער
פֿאַר װאָס האָבן זיך אױגן
באַגעגנט װי שׂונאים,
װי שװערדן די װערטער?

אין די װיסטע נעכט,
פֿון דיר פֿאַרפֿרעמדט,
שרײַט מײַן האַרץ נאָך דיר,
װי אין אַ שטאָט, װאָס ברענט,
דער רוף פֿון געשלײַדערטע גלאָקן,
װילד זיך יאָגנדיק. אױף טױט דערשראָקן.

46

"HEARING YOUR STEP AND ALARMED"

Hearing your step and alarmed—
I did not recognize my own voice.

Oh my beloved, my longed-for one,
in monstrous sorrow
why have eyes
met like enemies,
words like swords?

In the gloomy nights,
estranged from you,
my heart cries out for you,
as in a burning city
the call of tolling bells
rush wildly, afraid of death.

דאָס אַלץ איז װײט שױן אַװעק,

מײַן גאָלד, מײַן גאָלד, מײַן גאָלד,

װי אַ פֿאַרכּישופֿטער בֿרעג

אין זוניקן נעפּל, מײַן גאָלד.

פֿליִען אָן שעהען אַ מאָל,

הײב איך די אױגן ניט אױף,

הער װידער דעם בײג פֿון דײַן קול

און פֿאָלג און גיי אױף דײַן רוף,

און בין פֿאַרװירט און גערירט,

מאָדנע געריִרט און באַצױװנגען

פֿון ערינערונגען

ליכטיק און בלײך

און װי אַ הױך,

אַזוי װײַך.

"ALL THIS IS ALREADY LONG GONE"

All this is already long gone,

my gold, my gold, my gold,

like an enchanted shore

in a sunny haze, my gold.

The hours sometimes fly at me,

I do not raise my eyes,

hear again the inflection of your voice

and obediently follow your call,

am perplexed and overcome,

strangely touched and shaken

by memories

bright and pale

and, like a breath of air,

so gentle.

געוווען איז אפֿשר דאָס מײַן גליק:

פֿילן ווי דײַנע אויגן

האָבן זיך פֿאַר מיר געבויגן.

ניין, געוווען איז דאָס מײַן גליק:

גיין שווײַגנדיק הין און הער

מיט דיר איבערן סקווער.

ניין, ניט דאָס, ניט דאָס, נאָר הער:

ווען איבער אונדזער פֿרייד

פֿלעגט שמייכלענדיק זיך אײַנבייגן דעם טויט.

און אַלע טעג זײַנען געוווען פֿורפֿורן,

און אַלע שווער.

50

"PERHAPS THIS WAS MY HAPPINESS"

Perhaps this was my happiness:
To feel how your eyes
bowed down before me.

No, rather this was my happiness:
To go silently back and forth
across the square with you.

No, not even that, but listen:
How over our joy
there hovered the smiling face of death.

And all the days were purple,
and all were hard.

פֿון אַ בריוו

דער שטױביקער װעג,
די פֿאַרשיקורטע טריט...
אײנציקער מײַנער,
איך געדענק עס ניט.

די דעמערונג װי מאַסן בלומען,
די דעמערונג װי אָקטאָבער-װאַלד,
װען ער איז געקומען.

דער שטױביקער װעג,
דאָס פֿעלד נאָכן שניט,
די װאַקליקע טריט...
אָן אַ סוף, אָן אַ ברעג
איז געװואַקסן דאָס גליק...
ליכטיקער מײַנער,
איך געדענק עס ניט.

FROM A LETTER

The dusty road,
the drunken steps. . .
My one and only,
I don't remember.

Dusk, like masses of flowers,
dusk, like October woods,
when he came.

The dusty road,
the fields after harvest,
the tottering steps. . .
Without end, without limit.
Happiness grew . . .
My radiant one,
I don't remember.

איך גיי אין שאָטן פֿון דײַן לעבן
מיט ליבכטע פֿאָלגעדיקע טריט.
מײַן סוד איז פֿאַרהאַנגען און געהיט
אין מײַנע אָפֿגעװענדטע אויגן.

און פֿאָר דײַן בליק דעם ליכטיק־שטילן
בייג איך זיך, װי אַ װײַב און קינד,
און טו דײַן קלוגן העלן װילן,
און יעדע נאַכט רופֿט מיך דער װינט.

און צוקט בײַ טאָג אין פֿרומען שמייכל,
און פֿלאַטערט אויף אין װאָרט און צינדט.
געטרײַער מײַנער, זײַ מיר מוחל,
װען איך װעל װאָגלען מיט דעם װינט.

"I WALK IN THE SHADOW"

I walk in the shadow of your life
with light and docile steps.
My secret is veiled and guarded
by my averted eyes.

Before your quiet bright glance
I bow, like wife or child,
and do your sensible, clear will,
but every night the wind calls me.

And fidgets by day in pious smiles,
flutters off in words and burns.
Devoted one, forgive me
when I go wandering with the wind.

ליד

דײַן דינער פּראָפֿיל,
דײַן שמייכל פֿאַלש און געטרײַ.
און דער טאָג איז בלוי און פֿראַגיל,
ווי פֿאַרצעלײַ.

אַלץ, וואָס איך האָב געהאָפֿט,
אַלץ, וואָס דו האָסט פֿאַרגעסן,
קומט איצט צוריק אומפֿאַרהאָפֿט,
פֿאַרשפּינט אונדז אין זוניקע נעצן,

וויגט אונדז, פֿאַרוויגט אודז און צינדט,
ווי אַ גלוטיקער טרונק,
און אַקסלען שפּילן מיט ווינט,
מיט ערינערונג.

לינדן קוקן נאָך קיל,
פֿליסטערן און פֿאַרלעצן:
דער כּישוף איז שטיל און פֿראַגיל,
ווידער וועט ער פֿאַרגעסן.

56

POEM

Your thin profile,

your smile false and true.

The day is fragile and blue,

like porcelain.

Everything I'd hoped for,

everything you've forgotten,

returns now, hopeless,

enmeshes us in sunny nets.

Rocks us, lulls us, and warms us

like a glowing drink,

shoulders play in the wind

with memory.

Lindens still look cool,

whisper and snap:

The magic is quiet and fragile,

again, he'll forget.

געקושט מיין האַנט און זיך אַרומגעקוקט,

צי ס'זעט ניט קיינער.

פֿון גרויסער ליבע האָט דײַן קול געצוקט,

און האָסט זיך פֿאַרזיכטיק דאַן אָפּגערוקט,

ווען ס'איז פֿאַרבײַגעגאַנגען איינער.

"דער טאָג, מײַן טײַערער, געווען איז שיין,

צו שיין, צו גוט צוריקצוקערן..."

און ס'איז דײַן יעדעס וואָרט געווען

פֿול מיט פֿאַרטרויען און באַגערן.

און ווען עס האָבן אויפֿגעלויכטן ווײַך די ערשטע שטערן,

האָסטו פֿאַרריקט דײַן הוט, וואָס איז געזעסן קרום,

האָסטו געזעגנט זיך גערירט און שטום

און זיך אַוועקגעשאַרט בנעימות-פֿרום

אין דײַן פֿאַרשאָלטענער היים.

ליבערשט וואָלט איך וועלן דו זאָלסט שיכורן,

זאָלסט זיך וואַלגערן מיט גאַסנפֿרויען.

KISSED MY HAND

Kissed my hand and looked around,

to see if anyone had noticed.

Your voice quavered with passion

as you carefully moved away

when someone came by.

"My dear, the day was beautiful,

too beautiful, too pleasant to turn back . . ."

And every word you uttered

was full of confidence and desire.

When the first stars shone softly,

you straightened your hat, which sat awry,

bade an emotional and silent farewell

and slunk off with pious grace

to your accursed home.

I'd rather you were drunk

and carousing with women of the streets.

ניין, גאָרניט זאָגן.

נאָר אין ליכטיקייט,

אין לויטער פֿרײדיקייט

זיך אַראָפּבויגן

צו דעם צער אין דײַנע אויגן,

צו דער שולד אין דײַנע אויגן

און דיר זאָגן...

ניין, גאָרניט זאָגן.

60

"NO, THERE'S NOTHING TO SAY"

No, there's nothing to say.

Only in radiance,

in sheer joy

to bow down

to the grief in your eyes,

to the guilt in your eyes

and say to you. . .

No, there's nothing to say.

אוראַלטע מערדערין נאַכט, שוואַרצע מוטער אין נויט, העלף מיר!

פֿאַרנאַר אים, פֿאַרשפּין אים, פֿאַרשלינג אים, דערשלאָג אים צום טויט!

און איך,

וואָס טרערן זײַנען געווען מײַן געטראַנק,

און שאַנד מײַן ברויט,

וועל טרינקען פֿאַרחלשט,

גיריק און לאַנג,

ווי אַ ליבעס-געזאַנג,

זײַן ווײַבס געוויין,

דאָס שווײַגן פֿון קינדער,

דאָס פֿליסטערן פֿון פֿרײַנד

נאָך זײַן געביין.

וועל אויפֿשטיין ווי אײַנע, וואָס איז לאַנג געווען קראַנק,

אַ שוואַרץ געשפּענסט אין מאָרגנרויט,

וועל זיך בוקן צו אַלע פֿיר עקן פֿון רוים

און זינגען, און זינגען, און זינגען צום לעבן

אַ לויב פֿאַרן טויט.

62

"PRIMEVAL MURDERESS NIGHT"

Primeval murderess night, dark mother of necessity, help me!

Seduce him, ensnare him, swallow him, hound him to death!

And I,

whose drink was tears,

whose bread was shame,

will drink myself senseless,

greedily and long,

as on a love song,

on his wife's wailing,

the silence of his children,

the whispering of his friends

over his corpse.

I will arise like someone who was long ill,

a black spectre in the crimson dawn,

I will bow down to the four corners of the earth

and sing, and sing, and sing to life

a hymn to death.

ווען איך גיי מיט מײן ליבן דורכן טויִקן אַוונט פֿון פֿרילינג,

שמייכל ניט, פֿרעמדער, ווי איינער וואָס ווייסט,

אַז מיך ליבט ניט מײן ליבער.

ווײל טיף הענגט די נאַכט איבער מײנע פֿאַרטונקלטע אויגן.

און עס שפּרייטן זיך סאַמעטן-ווייך אין דער נאַכט

די שטיינערנע וועגן.

און פֿול מיט מיטלייד און פֿול מיט ליבשאַפֿט,

מיט ביטערע ליפֿן מיך קושנדיק

האָט איבער מיר דאָס אומגליק

זיך אָנגעבויגן.

64

"WHEN I WALK WITH MY BELOVED"

When I walk with my beloved through the misty spring evening,

don't smirk, stranger, as if you knew

that my lover doesn't love me.

Because the night hangs heavy over my darkened eyes.

And the stony road extends

satin-soft into the night.

Full of sympathy and full of love,

kissing me with bitter lips,

unhappiness hovers

over me.

גייט אַ פֿרײַנד פֿאַרבײַ אונדז אין דער לערער גאַס,

ווערן מײַנע אויגן שאַרפֿער, גרויער.

איבער אונדזער בײַזן מזל מאַך איך שפּאַס

און לאָז ניד׳ריקער אַראָפּ דעם שלייער.

טיפֿער, אָוונטיקער, בלויער ווערט די גאַס.

מײַנע הייסע ווערטער ברענען אין דײַן אויער.

אין מײַן ליבע איז פֿאַראַן אַזוי פֿיל האַס,

אין מײַן האַס אַזוי פֿיל לוסט און טרויער.

66

"A FRIEND PASSES US"

A friend passes us in the empty street,
and my eyes become sharper, grayer.
I joke about our bad luck
and lower my veil.

The street becomes duskier, deeper, bluer.
My hot words burn in your ears.
My love is full of so much hate,
my hate so full of joy and sorrow.

מײַן ניט, איך האָב זיך געביטן.
דעם רויִקן שמײכל ניט גלויב.
איך בין אַ טיגערן מיטן בליק פֿון אַ טויב,
איך בין אַ קינזשאַל צווישן בליטן, —
זאָלסט זיך היטן.

אַ שעה קומט און באַלד איז זי אויס —
מיט אַ שמײכל, אַ מעסער, אַ רויז.
מײַנע ליפּן וועלן זיס זײַן און רויט.
מײַן האַנט וועט אַ טאַנץ טון, אַ פֿלי טון
און אויף אונדזער שענדלעכן טויט
לײגן זיך צערטלעך און גרויס.

68

"DON'T THINK THAT I'VE CHANGED"

Don't think that I've changed.
Don't believe that serene smile.
I am a tiger with the look of a dove,
I am a dagger among the flowers—
Watch out!

The hour arrives and is soon gone—
With a smile, a knife, a rose.
My lips will be sweet and crimson.
My hand will dance, will fly—
and rest tender and large
on our shameful death.

ס'איז דער וועג אזוי שטיל,

פערלדיק-גרוי, פערלדיק-קיל,

און די זון שפרייט אין דער הויך

בריקן פֿון רויזן, בריקן פֿון רויך.

ס'איז דאָס האַרץ אזוי שטיל,

דײַן שווער-הייסער בליק,

דאָס שיכּורע גליק

איז ניט דאָס, וואָס איך וויל.

ס'איז דאָס האַרץ אזוי שטיל

און קניט אין טונקעלן פֿאָרגעפֿיל,

און ציטערט און לײַדט

פֿון צו פֿיל פֿאַרשטיין, פֿון צו פֿיל צערטלעכקייט.

"THE ROAD IS SO STILL"

The road is so still,

pearl-cool, pearl-gray,

and the sun spreads on high

bridges of roses, bridges of smoke.

The heart is so still.

Your passionate gaze,

that drunken bliss

is not what I want.

The heart is so still,

kneeling in dark foreboding,

trembling and suffering

from knowing too much, feeling too much.

איך האָב ניט געוווּסט, מײַן ליבער,
אַז מיט לאַנגזאַמע בענקענדיקע פֿינגער
קריץ איך דיך אײַן אין מײַנע לידער.

איצט האָבן זיי דעם שווערן גלאַנץ
פֿון דײַנע אויגן, די שאַרפֿע ליניע
פֿון דײַן מויל, פֿון דײַן
עקשנותדיקער האַנט.

דאָס ווּנדער,
ווען מײַן אייגן וואָרט
באַרירט מיך מיט דײַן האַנט.

ווען נאָענט, אַ נאָענט וואַקסטו אַרויס
פֿון שטרענגן ליכטיקן אקאָרד.

דאָס ווּנדער...

72

"I DID NOT KNOW, MY DEAR"

I did not know, my dear,

that my slow, yearning fingers

had engraved you into my poems.

Now they have the hard sheen

of your eyes, the sharp line

of your mouth, of your

stubborn hand.

The wonder:

that my own word

stirs me with your hand.

When near, oh near, you emerge

out of the harsh, musical notes.

The wonder. . .

אַזוי ווי מײַן בליק דער פֿאַרטערערטער

איז דער אָוונט בלוי און אינטים.

זאָג דײַנע קאַלטע ווערטער,

נאָר מיט אַ צערטלעכער שטים.

און אין דײַן שטים דאָ און דאָרטן

וועט אויפֿבליען אומגעריכט

אין לבֿנה-שײַן אַ גאָרטן,

אין לבֿנה-שײַן אַ געזיכט.

און דאָס טרויערשפיל ווידער

פֿון אַ קראַנקן געוויסן,

איך ווייס אַזוי פֿיל, מײַן מידער,

אָ, איך וויל מער ניט וויסן.

נאָר הערן אַזוי-אַ ביז שפעט

דעם שאָטן פֿון ליבע קומען,

טרויעריק ווי טשערעט,

צאַרט ווי די נעמען פֿון די בלומען.

74

"JUST LIKE MY TEARFUL GAZE"

Just like my tearful gaze

the evening is blue and intimate.

Speak your cold words,

but with a gentle voice.

Your voice, here and there

will unexpectedly blossom

into a garden in the moonlight,

a face in the moonlight.

And that sad game again

of a guilty conscience.

I know it so well, my weary one,

oh, I don't want to know more.

But listen, just like this, until late

to the shadow of love coming,

sadly, like river grasses,

gently, like the names of flowers.

איז די גאָלדענע פּאַווע געפֿלויגן, געפֿלויגן,
און די נאַכט האָט געעפֿנט די גאָלדענע אויגן.
ליכטיקער מײַנער, שלאָף אײַן.

די נאַכט האָט געעפֿנט די גאָלדענע אויגן,
בין איך פֿידל געוואָרן און דו דער בויגן.
אומרויִקער מײַנער, שלאָף אײַן.

בין איך פֿידל געוואָרן און דו דער בויגן,
און דאָס גליק איבער אונדז האָט פֿאַרליבט זיך געבויגן.
צערטלעכער מײַנער, שלאָף אײַן.

און דאָס גליק איבער אונדז האָט פֿאַרליבט זיך געבויגן,
געלאָזט אונדז אַליין און פֿאַרפֿלויגן, פֿאַרפֿלויגן.
טרויעריקער מײַנער, שלאָף אײַן.

"THE GOLDEN PEACOCK FLEW OFF"

The golden peacock flew off and away,

and night opened its golden eye.

My radiant one, sleep on.

Night opened its golden eye,

I became the fiddle and you the bow.

My restless one, sleep on.

I became the fiddle and you the bow,

happiness arced fondly above us.

My gentle one, sleep on.

Happiness arced fondly above us,

left us alone, flew off and away.

My mournful one, sleep on.

SEALED LIPS

פֿאַרלאָשענע ליפּן

Farloshene lipn

_____

שדים האָבן אומעטיק געפֿײַפֿט

איך בין אַרײַן אין גאָרטן ווי אין אַ ווילדן וואָלקן.
שדים האָבן אומעטיק געפֿײַפֿט.
שטערן האָבן בלוטיק, פֿלאַצנדיק גערײַפֿט.

עס זײַנען פֿאַרבעיגעפֿלויגן פֿיל שפֿאָטנדיקע אויגן.
שטימען האָבן גליטשיק, שלאַנגיק מיך געשטרײַפֿט.
אַ שמאָל פֿלאַמענדיק מויל האָט אַ-ז-וי לאַנגזאַם צו מיר זיך צוגעבויגן.
שדים האָבן אומעטיק געפֿײַפֿט.

DEMONS WHISTLED SADLY

I went into the garden as into a wild cloud.

Demons whistled sadly.

As stars burst open, fierce and ripe.

Hordes of mocking eyes flew past.

Slippery voices, snakelike, stripped me.

A small, flaming mouth bent close to me, oh-so-slowly.

Demons whistled sadly.

פֿון מײַן פֿינצטערניש

1

איך רעד שטאַמלענדיק.

אין טױטלעכער אַנגסט

מיט זיך אַלײן זיך ראַנגלענדיק

זוך איך דאָס װאָרט,

װאָס זאָל אַרױסשטראַלן כאָטש קרום און בלאָס

מײַן פֿרײלעכן, מײַן װעלט-אַרומנעמענדן האַס.

2

די שאַרפֿע נעגל פֿון דעם טאָג האָבן אָפּגעלאָזט דעם קרבן.

אין דער פֿינצטערניש, צונױפֿגעדרײט,

און לעכערלעך, און קלײן,

ליג איך און הער, װי שטיל און רײן,

װי שטיל און ברײט

שטײגט אױף אין מיר אָן טרערן אַ געװײן

און שפּרײט זיך װי אַ ברײטער בריק צום מאָרגן.

82

OUT OF MY DARKNESS

1

I stammer.

In deadly anxiety

I wrestle with myself

searching for the word,

though twisted and pale, to radiate

my joyous, my all-encompassing hatred.

2

The day's sharp claws released their victim.

In the darkness, curled up,

ludicrous and small,

I lie and hear a still and pure,

a still and deep

tearless cry rise within me

and spreads like a broad bridge to the dawn.

3

ווי פֿון צעטראָטענע בלוטנדע טרויבן

פּרעסט מען אויס דעם איידעלן וויַין,

אַזוי האָב איך מיַין פֿרייד אויסגעזויגן

פֿון פּיַין,

און מיט גוססע הענט זי דערהויבן

צום בלענדנדן גרויזאַמען שיַין

פֿון גאָטס אויגן.

84

3

Just as delicate wine is pressed

from trampled, bloody grapes,

so I've sucked out my joy

from anguish,

and with dying hands raised it up

to the blinding, savage radiance

of God's eyes.

דאָס איז די נאַכט

דאָס איז די נאַכט, דער טרויער, דאָס ניט-וואָרן,

פֿון טרוימען דער פֿאַררעטערישער שײַן.

אומגליקלעכע, וואָס וועט זײַן?

זײ קאַלט, זײ קלוג. קער אָפּ זיך פֿון די שטערן,

פֿון קינדערשפּיל מיט שאָטנס, טוי און דופֿט,

זײַ שטיל, זײַ שטיל,

און מיטן גאַנצן פֿרירנדיקן בלוט וועסטו דערהערן,

ווי עס עפֿנט זיך די ערד

און ווי דער וואָרעם רופֿט.

86

THIS IS THE NIGHT

This is the night, the sadness, the non-existence,

the treacherous glow of dreams.

Unhappy one, what will be?

Be cold, be clever, turn away from the stars,

from child's play with shadows, dew and fragrance,

be still, be still,

and with all your congealing blood you will hear,

how the earth opens

and the worm beckons.

שלאַנקע שיפֿן

שלאַנקע שיפֿן דרימלען אויפֿן געשוואָלן גרינעם וואַסער,
שוואַרצע שאָטנס שלאָפֿן אויפֿן קאַלטן האַרץ פֿון וואַסער.
אַלע ווינטן זײַנען שטיל.
כמאַרעס רוקן זיך געשפּענסטיק אין דער נאַכט דער שטומער.
בלייך און רויִק וואַרט די ערד אויף בליץ און דונער.
איך וועל זײַן שטיל.

SLENDER SHIPS

Slender ships drowse on swollen green water,

black shadows sleep on the cold heart of water.

All the winds are still.

Clouds shift like ghosts in the speechless night.

The earth, pale and calm, awaits thunder and lightning.

I will be still.

דו האַרטע, האַרישע שטים, ווער שטילער.

איר שאַרפֿע און דאָרשטיקע אויגן — אַרונטער

די טונקעלע ווִיעס. און זאָלן אין רויִקן צער

די ווִיסע פֿאַרלאַנגענדע הענט

אין שויס זיך פֿאַרפֿלעכטן.

און וואַרט.

אַ, לײכט, זײער לײכט, אַ כישופֿדיק צאַרט

וועט דער אָוונט מיט לופֿטיקע, גיפֿטיקע פֿינגער

באַרירן דײן לײב, שטאָלצע פֿרוי,

דײן מויל און דײן בליק און די שטורמישע האָר,

און מאָלן זיי גרוי,

און פֿינצטער און פֿלינק

אַרום דײן אײנזאַמקייט קריצן אַ ריזיקן רינג.

זײ שטילער און שטילער. אַזוי... אָט אַזוי...

ס'איז גאָרניט געווועזן. ס'איז אַלץ שוין פֿאַריבער.

90

QUIETLY

You hard, masterful voice, be still.

You sharp, thirsting eyes—lower

your dark lashes. In calm sorrow

let the white demanding hands

lie folded in your lap.

And wait.

Oh lightly, so lightly, oh magically, tenderly

the evening will stir your body

with light, poisoned fingers, proud woman,

your mouth, your gaze, your disheveled hair,

and paint them gray

and dark and nimble,

etching a mighty ring round your loneliness.

Quietly, quietly, like this . . . just like this. . .

Nothing happened. Everything is already past.

אָפֿט גיי איך ווי הינטער אַ שלייער,

און עס מישט זיך מײַן טראָט מיט די טריט

פֿון אײַך, ניט-געזעענע גייער,

טרויעריק-שיינע, בלוט און צווייט

פֿון מײַן וואַנזיניקן פֿרילינג.

און איבער רוישנדע גאַסן

טראָג איך אין וואַכן געמיט

אײַערע שטימען, שמייכלען, גרימאַסן,

ווי מען טראָגט אויף די ליפֿן אַ ליד,

ווי אויפֿן פֿינגער אַ קאָסטבאַרן רינג.

92

"OFTEN I WALK AS IF BEHIND A VEIL"

Often, I walk as if behind a veil,
my steps mingling with yours
unseen travelers,
sadly beautiful, blood and flowers
of my demented springtime.

Cautiously, I carry
your voices, smiles, grimaces
through raw, rushing streets
as one carries a song on one's lips,
or a costly ring on one's finger.

טריוויאַלים

זיי קײַקלען זיך פֿאַרבײַ
אין גרינעם שטראַל פֿון דער היסטעריישער לבֿנה
און טונקלען זיך,
די דינע פּיסלעך אונטער זיך,
אין אַלע שאַטנדיקע ווינקלען.

און זײַנען גוט.
און זײיערע לאַנגע, שוואַרצע שלאַנגיש אויסגעקרימטע פֿינגער
טײַטלען אַלץ אויף דיר,
און ציִען זיך פֿאַמעלעך אַלץ צו דיר, צו דיר,
און זײַנען גוט.

און דו, מענטש, וואָס ציטערסטו?
דו אינדזל שלאַנקער צווישן שטײַגנדיקע כוואַליעס,
דו שמאַלער בליץ, וואָס לעשט זיך צווישן כמאַרעס,
דו פֿון גאָטס האַנט געשלײַדערטער קונזשאַל,
מיט זונשײַן אָנגעגאָסענער באָקאַל,
צעשמעטערט פֿון דער נאַכט —
דו נאַר, דו נאַר, דו אָרעמער נאַר, אין טיפֿער נאַכט,
אין דראָענדיקן שײַן פֿון דער היסטעריישער לבֿנה.

94

DEMONS

They roll by
in the green rays of the hysterical moon
and grow dark,
their spindly legs underneath them,
in all the shadowy corners.

And they are good.
Their long, black, snakelike, twisted fingers
pointing only at you,
stretching slowly to you, only to you,
and they are good.

And you, human being, why are you trembling?
You slender island among the rising waves,
you, thin spark extinguished among the clouds,
you, the outflung dagger from God's hand,
with your sunshine-filled goblet
shattered by the night—
You fool, you fool, you poor fool, in the deep of night,
in that menacing shimmer of the hysterical moon.

נאַכט

איך שלאָג זיך אין דער פֿינצטערניש מיט שׂונאים,
ניט זעענדיק קיין איינציק פנים.

און יעדע נאַכט אַ סוויסטשען און אַ קנאַלן,
אַ שטאַמפן פֿון פֿאַרשווינדנדיקע טריט.
און איך שטיי בלוטנדיק און טויטלעך-מיד
און וויל ניט, וייל ניט פֿאַלן.
און יעדע נאַכט דערנאָך דאָס ברייטע שטראָמענדיקע שווייגן
ווי פֿון פֿילע אָרגלען, און אויפֿגעכװאַליעט ליכט,
און איבער מײַנע אויגן,
שמייכלענדיק אַריבערגעבויגן,
אַ ריזיק שאָטנדיק געזיכט.

NIGHT

I battle enemies in the darkness,

not seeing a single face.

Every night, whistling and banging,

and the tramp of disappearing steps.

I stand bloodied and dead weary

but will not, will not fall.

Every night thereafter, the broad, enveloping silence

as from many pipe organs and restless lights,

and above me,

smiling, hovering,

an immense, shadowy face.

מיד

איך בין היינט מיד.
פֿאַרוווּנדעט פֿון די שאַרפֿע שטימען,
פֿון עמעצנס צו גוטן בליק.
און איך האָב דערהערט אַ וואָרט,
וואָס גליט אין מיר און גליט.

אַזוי מיד.

טונקל שפּרייטן זיך אין צימער
שאָטנס פֿון דער נאַכט
אויף וועלקן אָוונטרויט.
איך האָב היינט לאַנג געטראַכט
פֿון טויט.

די שטילקייט אין מיין צימער
איז ווי דער אָנריר פֿון שוואַרצן סאַמעט.
דער שימער אין די שוואַרצע וואַסערן פֿון שפּיגל
איז ווי שוואַרצער גלאַנץ פֿון סאַמעט.

אין וואַסער, זאָגט מען, איז גאָר גרינג דער טויט.

אַזוי מיד.

98

WEARY

I am weary today.
Wounded by the sharp voices
of someone's excessive gaze.
But I hear a word
that glows in me and glows.

So weary.

Darkness spreads over the room,
shadows of the night
on faded, evening red.
Today, I thought a long time
about death.

The silence in my room
is like the touch of black velvet.
The gloss on the heavy waters of the mirror
is like the black gleam of velvet.

In water, they say, it's quite easy to die.

So weary.

ליבע מאָנסטרען, האָט געדולד.

ס'איז ניכטערער טאָג, ס'איז די וועלט איבערפֿולט

מיט שײן און געװיש ביז די וױיטסטע זוניקע ברעגן.

איך גײ צוױשן מענטשן, איך גײ איבער פֿרײנדלעכע װעגן

דאַנקבאַר,   װוּנדערלעך פֿון אײך באַפֿרײט

איר זײַט װײַט,

װי אין גאַסן דער טראַמף פֿון אַרמײען,

געהערט אין שטילן פֿאַרחלומטן הױז,

װי אין אָפּגעלײגטע אַלײען

סילועטן, געזעען

דורכן גאָלדענעם נעפּל פֿון לאַמפּן בלױז,

נאָר עפּעס אין זשעסט און לאַנג דערמאָנט,

אַז אומהיימלעך זײַנען זײ דיר באַקאַנט.

ליבע מאָנסטרען, האָט געדולד.

װײַל נאַכט קומט, און דאָס האַרץ, קראַנק פֿון אַן אַלטער שולד,

אומבאַשיצט און אַלײן הערט גענענען די טריט,

הערט און װאַרט און װערט זיך ניט.

און איר זײַט דאָ! און עס צערינט דאָס צימער.

איך פֿאַרזינק צוױשן אײך, אַן אומגעניטער שװימער,

און װער צעטראַמפלט און צעקרימט.

איר זײַט אַזױ שרעקלעך און דאָך אומבאַשטימט.

איר װאַקסט װי בערג אַרום מיר, װי ריזיקע הינט,

DEAR MONSTERS

Dear monsters, be patient.

It's sober day, the world is overflowing

with light and sound to its farthest sunny shores.

I walk among people, along friendly roads

gratefully, wonderfully free of you.

You are distant,

like the tramp of armies in the streets

heard in the quiet, dreamy house,

something in my gesture and my gait is recalled

as silhouettes seen only

through the golden haze of lamplight

in remote avenues

but weirdly familiar to you.

Dear monsters, be patient.

Because night comes and the heart, sick with an old guilt,

hears the approaching steps defenceless and alone,

hears and waits and resists.

Now you are here! And the room dissolves.

I sink among you, an inexperienced swimmer,

and am trampled and deformed.

You are so terrible and yet so vague.

You loom around me like mountains, like giant hounds,

און מיט מיר צוזאַמען ווייעט איר בלינד,
צוזאַמען מיט מיר ברומט איר טעמפּ און צעדולט
די מעשׂה פֿון אַן אַלטער, אַלטער שולד.
...עס וויינט דאָס האַרץ, ווי בלודנע שאָף,
און פֿאַרוויינט זיך צום קראַנקן שלאָף.

together with me you howl blindly,

together with me roar, dull and nagging,

the story of an old, old guilt.

. . .The heart weeps like a stray sheep,

weeps itself to sickly sleep.

די נאַכט איז אַריַין אין מיַין הויז

די נאַכט איז אַריַין אין מיַין הויז

מיטן געברום פֿון שטערן, וואַסערן, פֿליגל,

מיטן שיַין פֿון זומפֿן, שליאַכן, טומאַנען.

איך בין געלעגן שטאַר און פֿינצטער.

ביַימער זיַינען אַריַין אין מיַין הויז,

גערוקט זיך ריזיק מיט וואָרצלען און שטאַמען

און אָרטיפֿע בליקן פֿון בלעטער.

און וואָלקנס אויסטערל...-גרויס

זיַינען געקומען מיט דונער און לאַכן,

ווי טונקעלע קעפ פֿון די געטער.

און אַלע האָבן זיי געדרייט זיך שווער, און ווילד, און וויסט.

און אַלע האָבן זיי גערוישט: ''דו ביסט, דו ביסט, דו ביסט''.

איך בין געלעגן שטאַר און פֿינצטער.

104

NIGHT CAME INTO MY HOUSE

Night came into my house

with the roar of stars, flood, wings,

with the glow of swamps, dirt roads and mists.

I lay tense and miserable.

Trees came into my house,

looming gigantic with roots and trunks

and ancient deep glances from the leaves.

And huge, bizarre clouds

came with thunder and laughter,

like the dark heads of pagan gods.

And all of them swirled, hard and wild and bleak.

Clamoring: "You are, you are, you are".

I lay tense and miserable.

הַאָרט הָאָרץ

הַאָרט פֿאַראַכטנדיק הָאָרץ,

לאָז אַרײַן די ליכטיקע כוואַליע

פֿון זונות, מוטערס און קינדער,

בעטלערס, קריפּלס און טענצערס

און אַלטע לײַט פֿון דער שטאָט,

נאָר בלײַב ניט מיט זיך און מיט גאָט,

הַאָרט הָאָרץ,

אַנטלױף צו מענטשן פֿון גאָט.

HARD HEART

Hard, contemptuous heart,

let the bright wave in

of whores, mothers and children,

beggars, cripples and dancers

and old people from the city.

Don't remain only with yourself and with God.

Hard heart,

Flee from God to people.

דערצייל עס אים: זי האָט פֿאַרגעבן

זיך ניט געקענט איר טרויעריק געמיט,

איז זי געגאַנגען דורכן לעבן

מיט זיך אַנטשולדיקנדע טריט.

דערצייל, אַז זי האָט ביזן טויט

געשיצט געטרײַ מיט הױלע הענט

דאָס פֿײַער, װאָס איז איר געװען פֿאַרטרױט

און אין אײגענעם פֿײַער געברענט.

און װי אין שעהען פֿון איבערמוט

האָט זי מיט גאָט זיך שװער געװערט,

װי טיף געזונגען האָט דאָס בלוט,

װי צוװערגן האָבן זי צעשטערט.

108

EPITAPH

Tell him: she couldn't forgive herself
for her despondent mood,
so she went through life
with self-effacing steps.

Say that until her death
she faithfully protected with bare hands
the flame entrusted to her
and in that same fire she burned.

And how in hours of exultation
she took God to task,
how her blood sang deeply
as dwarfs destroyed her.

שיינע ווערטער פֿון מאַרמאָר און גאָלד

שיינע ווערטער פֿון מאַרמאָר און גאָלד,
ניט אײַך, ניט אײַך האָב איך געוואָלט.

פֿאַר וואָר, איך האָב די לידער ניט געוואָלט.

נאָר אַנדערע — ווי פֿײַער און ווי פֿרײַלעכער שטורעם,
וואָס צערײַסן אימפּעטיק דעם דורכזיכטיקן פֿורעם.

צו שפּעט.

און איך וואָלט וועלן זײַן אַנדערש צו מענטשן.
נאָר אױך איצט בין איך ניט גרייט
ליב צו האָבן קינד און קייט.

אָבער ווען איך וואָלט קענען פֿאַרגעבן
מײַן פֿאַרפּײַניקט לעבן
און צוגיין צו דעם און צו יענעם,
די שלעכטע, די שיינע, די פֿון חלום געצוונדן,
וועלט-פֿאַרלירער, וועלט-וואַגאַבונדן,
און זאָגן: "איך וויל זיך אײַך געבן.
איך וויל זיך פֿאַרשוועדן,
ווי הייליקע אין לעגענדן.
זאָל מײַן גוטסקייט אויפֿגיין איבער אײַך
שײַנענדיק און רײַך..."

110

BEAUTIFUL WORDS OF MARBLE AND GOLD

Beautiful words of marble and gold,
it wasn't you, wasn't you I wanted.

In fact, I didn't want these poems.

But others—like fire and joyful storms
that swiftly shred the transparent forms.

Too late.

I wanted to be different to people.
But even now I'm not ready
to love kin and kind.

But if I could forgive
my tormented life
and approach this one and that one,
the bad ones, the good ones, those lit by dreams,
losers of the world, vagabonds,
and say: "I want to give myself to you.
I want to squander myself.
Like the holy saints of legend,
may my goodness rise over you
glowing and rich . . ."

צו שפּעט.

איך הער אָפֿט אומהיימלעכע טריט.
איך טראַכט אָפֿט וועגן לעצטן exit
און איך שווער
בײַ עלזאַ לאַסקער שילער, רילקע און באָדלער
אַז איך וועל שטומען, ניט קלאָגן.

די לעצטע באַלײידיקונג פֿון לײַב וועל איך ווירדיק פֿאַרטראַגן.
וועל אין יענע שעהנע אפֿשר חלומען, אפֿשר וואַקסן
זען וועלטן זיך דרייען אַרום די אַקסן,
און מײַן היים אין מאָרגנרויט, און פֿעלדער אין דרימל,
און ווי אין אַ שטאָט, וואָס פֿרייט זיך און בליט,
מײַן אומעטיק קינד קניט.
איך וועל אַ צי טון מיט די אַלץ נאָך שײַנע אַקסלען,
וועל די ציטערנדע ליפֿן אפֿשר נאָך צוויינגען
צו שמייכלען, און עס וועט מיר געלינגען.
און שמייכלענדיק, און אָטעמלאָז
קעגן דער אומגעהויערער אײַזערנע מאַסקע פֿון הימל
לאָזן דעם שוואַכן רויך פֿון לעצטן פּאַפּיראָס.

112

Too late.

Often, I hear weird footsteps.
Often, I think about the last exit
and I vow
by Elsa Lasker Schüler, Rilke, and Baudelaire,
that I will be silent, not lament.

I will tolerate with dignity the last insult of the flesh.
In those hours I will perhaps dream, perhaps grow,
see worlds rotating on their axes,
my home in the red dawn, drowsing fields,
as in a happy and blooming city
my sad child kneels down.
I will shrug these still beautiful shoulders,
I will, perhaps, still force these trembling lips
to smile and I will succeed.
Smiling and breathless
I exhale the weak smoke of my last cigarette
to the enormous iron mask of the heavens.

SUN, ASPHALT, ROADS

זון, אַספֿאַלט, װעגן

Zun, asfalt, vegn

———————————————————

אין הייסן שאַרפֿן גלאַנץ פֿון טיפֿן ווילדן גאָרטן,

ווו ווערבעס הענגן בלייך און סאָסנעס וואָלקן-טונקל,

ווו טולפֿן פֿלאַקערן ווי גאָלד און ווי גאַרפֿונקל,

אין זון-דורכשטראַלטן, זון-באַרוישטן גאָרטן

שמידט דער הייִשעריק דעם האַרבסט.

אַ פֿראַסטיק, האַסטיק ליד שטײַגט אויף יונגע גראָזן

און האַמערט אין די בליִענדיקע ביימערשפּיצן,

און פֿייגל זון-באַזוימטע וויגן זיך און בליצן.

אין שטילע, ציטערדיקע, ברענענדיקע גראָזן

שרײַט דער האַרבסט.

AUTUMN

In the hot sharp glare of that dense wild garden,

where willows droop listlessly and pine trees darkly clouded

where tulips sparkle like gold and like garnets—

in that sunshine-streaming, sun-intoxicated garden

the locust forges autumn.

An impetuous, icy song rises from the new grasses;

throbs in the flowering tree-tops,

birds, sun-drenched, streak and soar.

In the silent, trembling, burning grasses;

autumn shrieks.

איבער ברוינע דעכער

איבער ברוינע דעכער רויטער שײַן.
און בלינדע שויבן ווי פּערל אין ווײַן.
איבער טונקעלע גאַסן בייגט זיך די רו.
מײַן ווײַטער דו.

איבער טונקעלע גאַסן בייגט זיך די רו.
ברענען ווי טרערן די פֿײַערן מיד.
אויף טעלעגראַף-סטרונעס צעווייגט זיך אַ ליד:
דו, דו...

OVER BROWN ROOFS

Crimson glows over the brown roofs.
The blinded panes are like pearls in wine.
Calm hovers over the darkened streets.
My distant you.

Calm hovers over the darkened streets.
The fires banked, burning like tears.
A song lilts on the telegraph poles:
You, you. . .

אָ, פֿלאַמענדיקע גערטנער ביי דעם ראַנד פֿון הימל,
צעפֿאַטלטע איריסן, יונגער בעז און מאָן,
און שווערע טונקל-גאָלדענע און טרויעריקע רויזן
און די בלויע בלום.

און גאַסן גרוי-לילאַ ווי פֿליגל פֿון טויבן.
די טיפֿע אויגן פֿון זאַכן שליסט חלום און דרימל.
און מענטשן ווערן טונקעלע און טרויעריקע רויזן,
און די ערד ווערט אַ שאָטן פֿון הימל.

120

EVENING

Oh, flaming gardens at the edge of the sky,
disheveled irises, young lilacs and poppies,
and heavy, sad, darkly golden roses
and blue blossoms.

Violet-grey streets like the wings of doves.
Deep-eyed objects locked in dream and drowsing.
People become dark and sad roses,
and the earth becomes a shadow of the heavens.

זון

איך ווייס, אַז די זון איז גאָטס גאָלדענע מאַסקע.

אָפֿט ווער איך רויִק און גוט,

ווען שגעון און עקל יאָגט דורך מײַן בלוט —

גאָט שמייכלט צו מיר פֿון הינטער זײַן מאַסקע.

עס טרעפֿט, אַז אין שווערן גרין-גאָלדענעם גאָרטן

הענגט די זון, ווי אַ פֿרוכט אויפֿן בוים.

דערפֿילט האָב איך דאָרטן

איין מאָל אין אַ ליכטיקער שעה

איר זאַפֿט אין מײַן מויל.

און אַ מאָל פֿאַר נאַכט אויפֿן ים

איז זי אַ פֿײַערדיקער שוואַן.

אַ ווײַסע און אַ גלײַכע

מיט אַ זילבערנעם האָרן צווישן די ליפֿן

בין איך אויף איר רוקן איין מאָל געריטן.

122

SUN

I know that the sun is God's golden mask.

Often, I become calm and agreeable

as madness and disgust rush through my blood—

God smiles at me from behind His mask.

Sometimes, in the dense, golden green garden

the sun hangs like fruit on a tree.

There, in a bright hour

I once felt

its juice in my mouth.

And one evening on the sea

it became a fiery swan.

White and erect,

I once rode on its back

a silver horn between its lips.

הַאַרבסט

דער צער פֿון פֿאַרגײן,
מײַן ליבער...

ווען מיר גײען
איבער די לאַנגע און לערע אַלײען,
און דײַן האַנט, ברוין און האַרבסטיק,
האַרבסטיק און מיד,
רוט אויף מײַן האַנט,
און מײַן בלוט בליט ניט,
און מײַן בלוט געדענקט דיך ניט...

מײַן ליבער,
דער סוד פֿון פֿאַרגײן...

איך מײן,
אז די ערד
אין איר לוסט צום פֿאַרגײן
האָט אונדז פֿאַרוואַנדלט אין שטיין.
צוויי גרויסע פֿינצטערע סטאַטוען
וואַנדלען לאַנגזאַם מיט שטײנערנע טריט
איבער טויטע אַלײען.

124

AUTUMN

The sorrow of passing,

my dear. . .

When we stroll down

the long and empty avenues,

and your hand, brown and autumnal,

autumnal and weary,

rests in my hand,

my blood does not flower,

my blood does not remember you. . .

My dear,

The secret of passing. . .

I think

that the earth

in her desire to turn

has transformed us into stones.

Two giant, dark statues

wandering slowly with stony tread

over dead avenues.

רעגן

1

אין זילבערנעם רעגן האָבן זיך בלומען געוויגט,

מיט אייגענעם דופֿט זיך באַרוישט און פֿאַרוויגט,

זיך לאַנגזאַם געבויגן

אונטער לאַנגע און לאַשטשענדע פֿינגער פֿון רעגן.

גראָזן האָבן צו דער ערד זיך געבוקט.

אין זילבערנעם רעגן האָבן זיך ביימער צעבליט

מיט בלייכע אָפֿאַלן אויף יעטוועדער בליט,

מיט לופֿטיקע קרוינען און לופֿטיקע שטאַמען,

ווי פֿאַרכּישופֿטע, זילבערנע, שלאַנקע פֿאַנטאַנען,

ווי אַ הויך געשווונגען און דורך טרערן געזונגען ליד.

2

דער טאָג איז וויאָלעט.

ווי וואָלקנס קוואַליען זיך גאַסן,

און קופֿער און בלוט פֿליסט אין שלאַנגישע פֿאַסן.

דער גאָלדענער לאָק פֿון אַ מיידל

צעוויגט זיך ווי זונשײַן אין נעפֿל,

און עס שווימען געזיכטער אַנטקעגן

ווײַט און אויסטערליש איידל,

און זיך פֿאַררוקט.

126

RAIN

1

In silvery rain the flowers sway,

lulled and cradled by their own fragrance,

slowly, they bend

under the long, caressing fingers of the rain.

Grasses bow to the earth.

In the silvery rain, trees burst into leaf,

every blossom a pale opal,

with airy crowns and cool trunks,

like spellbound, silvery, slender fountains,

like high-arcing song sung through tears.

2

The day is violet.

The streets are like turbulent clouds,

copper and blood flow in snakelike streams.

The golden tresses of a young girl

sway like sunshine in a mist,

and faces approaching, gliding,

distant, delicate, otherworldly,

blurring themselves.

ס'איז אַראָפּ אויף דער ערד הײַנט דער הימל,

עס גייען מענטשן זיך רויִק אין הימל,

רויִק, פֿון צער דורכגעצוקט.

The heavens fell to earth today,

people are calmly strolling in the sky,

calmly, trembling in sorrow.

ס'פֿאַלט דער האַרבסט אויף דער שטאָט און אויף מיר.

פֿינצטער האַרץ, שווײַג און באַוווּנדער:

זע, אַ נאַקעטער צווײַג מיט אַ בלאַט

בליט אין אַספֿאַלט צאַרט ווי אַ ליליע.

שווערער האַרבסט. שווערע טריט. איך בין אַלט.

פֿינצטער האַרץ מײַנס, ניט שעלט, גלייב אין וווּנדער:

ערגעץ-וווּ אין אַ שטאָט, אין אַ וועלט,

בלי איך איצט ווי אַ ליליע.

AUTUMN

Autumn descends on the city and on me.

Dark heart, be silent and marvel:

See how a naked branch with a leaf

flowers from the asphalt, gentle as a lily.

Heavy autumn, heavy steps, I am old.

Dark heart of mine, don't curse, believe in miracles:

Somewhere in the world, in a city

I am flowering like a lily.

דער שניי בליט היַינט אויף אַלע ביימער.

וואָס זשע ביסטו אומעטיק, מיַין שנייַיקע,

מיַין דערוויַיטערטע, נישט-דאָיקע?

די שמאָלע הענט אַראָפּגעלאָזן

און צוגעמאַכט די אויגן, די מימאָזן,

זיך איַינגעוויגט, זיך אָפּגעשלאָסן

צווישן שאָטנס שאַרכנדיקע,

אַ ליַיכטע און אַ האַרכנדיקע,

ווי אַ קליינער וויַיסער פֿויגל.

ווי דערשאָסענע שנייפֿייגל

פֿאַלט היַינט דער שניי פֿון אַלע ביימער.

132

SNOW

Snow blooms on all the trees today.

Why are you sad then, my snowy one,

my distant one, my absent one?

Whose slender hands are slack

the eyes, like mimosas, closed,

lulled and alone

among rustling shadows,

light and obedient,

like tiny white birds.

Like felled snowbirds,

the snow drops from all the trees today.

1

די אַלטע שטאָט, אַ שטאָט אי קליין אי גרוי,

איז טויט אַצינד ווי אַטען און ווי טראָי.

נאָר ליבנדיק, פֿאַרצערט, מיט וויַיכן אָטעם

כּישוף איך פֿון זיך אַרויס אַ מאָל איר שאָטן:

די גאַסן אין פֿאַמעלעכדיקן גאַנג אָן ווילן,

די שרעקיקע און אייביק פֿלוצלינגע אַפֿרילן,

די רעגנס פֿול מיט זון, די פֿעסטונג דראָענד-שטום,

די מידע פֿליגל פֿון צוויי אַלטע מילן.

די דעמבעס וואָנדערן אַרויס פֿון קייסער-סאָד,

דער רודער צוקט איבערן טיַיך, דער רודער שאָרכט: "אַ שאָד, אַ שאָד".

און ס'גענעצן די לייזדיקע בולוואַרן,

מעכטיק שטראָמט דער טיַי פֿון בלישטשענדיקע סאַמאָוואַרן,

איבער בענטשליכקט, תחינות, אייניקלעך —

אין אַן אָרגיע די שלײַפֿלעך פֿון די באָבעס,

און דינע ליפֿן שעפּטשעין אַלץ די נעמען פֿון די אָבות.

אויף טישן פֿינגער אין די בערד און אויפֿגעמישטער ש''ס

און ס'פֿלעכט דער ניגון זיך מיט אַ סטודענטס אַ באַס.

אין גערטלעך — זונבלומען, רעזעדע, מאָן,

בלאָנדע צעפּ, קאַקאַרדעס, פּושקין און נאַדסאָן.

און אין רויטער דעמערונג, מיט רייד אַלץ נעפּלדיקער, שטילער,

ווי נאָך אַן אומזיכטבאַרן פֿידל-שפּילער

BRISK (BREST-LITOVSK)

1

The old city, small and gray,

is dead now, like Athens and like Troy.

But lovingly, painfully, with soft breath

sometimes I conjure up her shadow:

the streets in slow gait, without will,

the scary and always sudden Aprils,

the rainstorms full of sun, the fortress menacingly still,

the weary wings of two old mills.

The oaks wandering out of the emperor's orchard,

the paddle drawing on the river, the paddle whispering: "A pity, a pity".

And the empty boulevards yawn.

Tea streams powerfully from sparkling samovars,

amid Sabbath candles, women's prayer books, grandchildren—

in an orgy of ribbons, the *bobes,*

thin-lipped, constantly whisper the names of the *oves.*

Fingering their beards, the sacred books open on tables

the melody blends with the basso of a student.

In the tiny gardens—sunflowers, rezedas, poppies,

blonde braids, beribboned cockades, Pushkin and Nadson.*

In the crimson dusk, talk mistier, quieter,

couples pair off into the fields.

* Russian poet Semyon Yakovlevich Nadson (1862–1887) dedicated one of his poems to
raise funds in aid of devastated Jewish communities.

135

ציִען פֿאַרלעך זיך אין פֿעלד.

און איבער אַלץ אַזוי פֿיל פֿרילינגדיקער טרויער, שימער,

דער ריח פֿון בעז.

2

יונגע פֿרויען ביי נאַכט אויף די שוועלן

רעדן פֿאַרטיפֿט און סטאַטעטשנע

וועגן די מענער אין דײַטשלאַנד,

וועגן ניט־גוטע,

וועגן ציגײַנער.

לאַנג שטײיען קינדער אין שאָטן,

פֿלאַטערן, האָפֿן,

אַז באַלד כאַפֿט זיי אַ ציגײַנער.

לויטער קליינע קלעאַפּאַטרעס,

פֿופֿצן־יעריקע פֿרײַלינס,

מיט העננטשקעס און פֿאַראַסאָלן

שווימען צירלעך איבער אַלײען,

ציִען אַרויף און אַראָפּ דעם וואַל,

הערן שטרענג ווערטער, וואָס קושן,

און ''אָונאָסי מאָיו דושו

וו טו טשודנויו דאָל...''*

בלענדנדע בײַטאָגן.

אַלע קרעמער דרעמלען.

אַלע גייער דרעמלען.

136

As if in tune with an invisible fiddler.

And over all this springlike sadness shimmers

the scent of lilacs.

2

Young women on the doorsteps in the evening

speak with solemn intensity

about their men in Germany,

about ghosts,

about gypsies.

Children stand a long time in the shadows,

aflutter and hoping

that soon a gypsy will spirit them away.

Innocent little Cleopatras,

fifteen-year-old frauleins

with gloves and parasols

glide ornamentally along the avenues,

raising and lowering their veils,

listening to strong words that kiss

and "carry off my soul

to the bright distance." *

Dazzling days.

Storekeepers drowsing.

Passersby drowsing.

אַ מאָל ווי אַ שטורעם

טראָגט זיך אַ צדיק

מיט שטראָפֿנדע ברעמען.

די גאַסן נייגן זיך

די בחורים

האַלטן דעם אָטעם אײַן.

אין הינטערגרונט סאָלדאַטן, אָפֿיצירן

מאַכן קאַליע

די ייִדישע לאַנדשאַפֿט.

אויפֿן האָרבאַטן שאָסיי

ווי אַ סאָבוויי דונערט

אַן איינזאַמער איזוואָשטשיק.

אָ, ווייכע זאַמדן פֿון מײַן שטאָט.

דעמבעס און טייַרויזן.

ווי דער ריח פֿון פֿריש ברויט

ווי דער ריח פֿון פֿריש ברויט

איז יעדן פֿרימאָרגן

אין אַלע גאַסן

און שטיבער

דײַן ''גוט מאָרגן!''

*''טראָג אַוועק מײַן נשמה אין ליכטיקער וועלט''.

138

Sometimes, a pious Jew

storms along

with chastising eyebrows.

Streets sway,

young men

hold their breath.

In the background

soldiers and officers

despoil

the Jewish landscape.

On the rutted highway

a lonely coach thunders

like a subway.

Oh, soft sands of my city.

Oaks and tea roses.

Like the smell of fresh bread

every day

in all the streets and houses

is your "good morning!"

bobes—grandmothers
oves—Biblical patriarchs, Abraham, Isaac, and Jacob

אַדעס

געדענקט איר, שיינער ריטער,
דעם פֿריילעכן פֿלאַטער-פֿליטער
פֿון שלייערן, אויגן און צעפ?

פֿלעגט איר דעם הויף נאָר פֿאַרבײגײן
אומבאַקאַנט, שלאַנק און פֿולקאָמען,
איבערן ראַנד פֿון באַלקאָנען
פֿלעגן מיידלעך זיך ציטערדיק נײגן.

אָ, טרױעריקער ריטער, געדענקט איר
אַ ליכטיקן שמאָלן אָוואַל
אין גאָלדענעם, בלענדנדן זאַל?
און אַ לאַטשענדן און אַ פֿאַרבענקטן
האַלב פֿאַרגעסענעם וואַלס
אויפֿן האַלב קינדישן באַל?

און אױף בולוואַרן, פֿאַרשפֿונען
אין שײַן פֿון עלעקטרישע זונען
האַלב געשוווועבט און האַלב געשוווומען
האָבן מיר, גאַנץ אין זיך פֿאַרשלאָסן.
און פֿון אָרקעסטער איז געפֿלאָסן
די פֿאַרחלומטער פֿאָפֿורי
און געבעטן: "בלי!"

140

ODESSA

Do you remember, handsome knight,
that happy flitter–flutter
of veils, eyes and braids?

When you passed by the courtyard
unknown, slim and perfect,
young girls would lean trembling
over the edges of the balconies.

Oh, sad knight, do you remember
a bright slender oval
in the dazzling, golden hall?
And a nostalgic, caressing,
half-forgotten waltz
at the youthful ball?

And a spinning on the boulevards
into the gleam of electric suns
half-gliding, half-floating
completely locked into ourselves
And from the band there lilted
the dreamy potpourri,
demanding: "Flower!"

און קענט איר זיך דערמאָנען

אַלץ דאָס, וואָס האָט ניט קיין נאָמען

און איז בלויז אַ דופֿט און אַ סוד?

און דעם אָטעם פֿון סטעפּ,

און פֿון זון, און פֿון סמאָלע?

און צום זינגענדן ים האָט די שטאָט,

ווי מיט אַ זײַדענעם שלעפּ,

געניידערט פֿון טויזנט מירמלנע טרעפּ.

And can you remember

everything that has no name

is only a fragrance, a mystery?

and a breath of the steppe,

of sun and of tar?

The city lowered,

as if by a silken cord,

down a thousand marble steps

into the singing sea.

ניט צופֿרידן

...און די מענטשן קוקן אויף מיר קרום,

אזוי אַז כאַטש נעם און צעוויין זיך...

איך בין ניט צופֿרידן מיט מײַן "פֿוירנישד רום",

איך בין ניט צופֿרידן מיט קיין זאַך.

געוויגט זיך הײַנט אויפֿן "סטראַפֿ" אין "על"

צום טאַקט מיט פֿאַרשווואַרצטע ייִדן.

ס'איז די נאַכט געווען שוואַרץ, ווי דאָס געמיט פֿון אַ קנעכט.

איך בין מיט די נעכט ניט צופֿרידן.

און די טעג זײַנען הייליק און געל,

ווי פּסוקים אין אַלטן סידור.

אפֿשר וואָלט מיר ניט געווען אזוי שלעכט,

ווען איך טרוים ניט קיין לידער.

144

DISCONTENTED

. . . And people look at me strangely,

so, go have a good cry . . .

I'm not happy with my furnished room,

I'm not happy with anything.

Swung back and forth today on the El strap

to the rhythm of worn-out Jews.

The night was dark as the mood of a slave,

I am not pleased with these nights.

And the days are holy and yellowed,

like the verses in an old prayer book.

Perhaps I would not be so disheartened

if I didn't dream of poems.

אין קאַפֿע

1

איצט אַליין אין קאַפֿע,

ווען עס לעשן זיך שטימען און וויאַנען,

ווען פֿערלדיק צינדט זיך לאָמפּן

און שווימען אַרויס פֿון קאַפֿע

ווי לויכטנדע שוואַנען

איבער דער גאַס —

— קעלנער, שוואַרצע קאַווע — דעמיטאַס.

איצט אַליין אין קאַפֿע,

ווען עס שאַרכן די רגעס ווי זײַד,

הייב איך אויף צו דער גאַס, צו דער וויַיט

מײַן שוואַרצן און דופֿטיקן וויַין.

און ווי אַ געזאַנג איז דער געדאַנק,

אַז ס'פֿאַלט פֿון מיר אין טונקלקייט

אַ ווײַסער שײַן.

2

און אַלע פּנימער אין רויך ווי מאַסקן.

אַ וויַיץ, אַן אַקסלצוק, אַ בליק אַ טריבער,

און פֿאַלשע ווערטער צינדן זיך, פֿאַרבלאַסן.

האָב איך דיר ווייי געטאָן, מײַן ליבער?

146

AT THE CAFÉ

1

Alone in the café now,

as voices hush and fade,

as lamps give off a pearly glow

and float out of the café

and over the street—

like luminous swans.

—Waiter, black coffee—demitasse!

Alone in the café now,

with moments rustling like silk,

I raise my dusky fragrant wine

to the street, to the distance.

And like a song is the thought

I give off into the gloom,

a white light.

2

All the faces in smoke, like masks.

A joke, a shrug, a bleak glance,

and false words flaring, making you blanch.

Have I offended you, my dear?

מיר טראָגן אַלע דאָ פֿאַראַכטלעך קאַלטע מאַסקן.

מיט קלוגער איראָניע פֿאַרשטעלן מיר דעם פֿיבער

און טויזנט שמייכלען, און געשרייען, און גרימאַסן.

האָב איך דיר וויי געטאָן, מײַן ליבער?

3

מיטן פּראָסטיקן שײַן פֿון די לאָמפּן

און בליקן, און שטימען

שווימט דיר אַקעגן מײַן שווײַגן —

אַ געהיימער און ליכטיקער סימן.

קרײַזט ווי אַ זומערוווינט אַרום דיר.

רעדט ציטערדיק צו דיר

וועגן דיר און מיר.

אָ, שטילע, שטילע ווערטער

וועגן דיר און מיר.

און שווײַגט.

און וויגט דיך מיט בענקענדע הענט.

און נעמט דיך מיט ווײַסע און צוקנדע הענט.

148

Here, all of us wear cold, contemptuous masks.

We disguise the fever with clever irony

and a thousand smiles, shouts and grimaces.

Have I offended you, my dear?

3

In the frosty gleam of the lamps

in the glances, in the voices

my silence floats towards you—

a bright and secret sign.

Wafts like a summer breeze around you,

speaks haltingly to you

about you and me.

Oh, quiet, quiet words

about you and me.

And becomes silent

lulls you with yearning hands.

Takes you with white and quivering hands.

מיידלעך אין קראָטאָנאַ פּאַרק

אין האַרבסטיקן פֿאַרנאַכט
האָבן מיידלעך זיך פֿאַרוועבט
ווי אין אַ וועלקן בילד.
זייערע אויגן זײַנען קיל, דער שמייכל ווילד און דין.
זייערע קליידער זײַנען לאַוונדער, אַלט-רויז און עפּל-גרין.
אין זייערע אָדערן פֿליסט טוי.
זיי האָבן ווערטער העלע און לערע.
זיי האָט אין טרוים געליבט באָטיטשעלי.

150

GIRLS IN CROTONA PARK

On autumn evenings

girls weave themselves

as in a faded portrait.

Their eyes are cool, their smiles wild and thin.

Their dresses lavender, old rose and apple-green.

Dew flows through their veins.

Their talk is bright and empty.

Botticelli loved them in his dreams.

פֿינפֿטע עוועניו, פֿאַר נאַכט

1

עס איז אַפּריל
און דער ריינער רוף פֿון אַ גלאָק.
אויף פֿיערדיקע הענט
הייבט די גאַס אויף
דעם שטאַרבנדן טאָג.

ווי שיין, ווי טרויעריק זײַנען אַלע געזיכטער.

עס איז דער טרויער פֿון אַפּריל,
און שוואַרצע פּראָצעסיעס פֿון אויטאָס,
פֿאַרבלייכטע דין רוישנדע קליידער,
און אויף מאַרמאָרנע טרעפּ פֿון האָטעל —
מענטשן איינגעפֿאַסט אין איידלשטיינער
פֿון איידל רויִק לײַכטנדיקע ליכטער.

2.

איבער דער אָוונטיקער עוועניו,
אין ליליענעם נעפּל פֿון דער עוועניו
האָבן פֿיערדיקע שמעטערלינגען
אויפֿגעפֿלאַטערט.

איבער דער עוועניו
שווימען,

152

EVENING ON FIFTH AVENUE

1

It's April

and the pure stroke of a bell.

The street is raised up

on fiery hands

to the ebbing day.

How beautiful, how sad, the faces are.

It is April's sorrow,

black processions of cars,

pale, lightly-rustling clothing,

and on the marble steps of the hotel—

people set like gemstones

of delicate, idyllic, shining light.

2

Over the dusky avenue,

in the violet mist of the avenue

iridiscent butterflies

flutter.

Limousines

float along the avenue

ווי פֿאָרסודעטע שיפֿן,

לימוזינען,

און עס הענגט דער פֿאַרצווייפֿלטער רוער געשריי פֿון סירענען

דראָענדיק.

טראָגנדיק נאַכט אין זייערע אויגן,

נאַכט און צעשטערונג און גאָלד אין די אויגן,

ווי לידער זיך וויגנדיק, גייען יונגע פֿרויען,

און שפּרייטן אויס נערוועז איבער דער עוועניו

זייערע קליינע פֿליגל

פֿון וואָנזיניקע שמעטערלינגען.

like mysterious ships,

and the raw shriek of sirens hangs

threateningly.

Carrying night in their eyes,

night and destruction and gold in their eyes,

like poems lulling themselves, young women stroll

and nervously spread their small wings

over the avenue

like demented butterflies.

דער אָוונט בליט. די גאַס רוישט העל ווי טויזנט קוואַלן.
עס שווימען פֿיִערן אַרויף פֿון זונשטויב און קאָראַלן.
וויטרינעס — פֿלאַמענדיקע היילן. וואַסערפֿאַלן
פֿון טיפֿן סאַמעט, זיַדנס שווער און קיל.
און מענטשן אין אומענדלעכן קאַדריל
באַגעגענען זיך און ווערן ווי פֿאַרפֿאַלן.
און ס'זוכן אויגן, אויגן זינגען, לאַכן,
אָבער מיר דאַכט, עס קניִען אַלע זאַכן.

בלוי בליט דער ווינט, בלויע שאָטנס פֿאַלן.
עס פֿליט אַ קאָר פֿאַרביַ אויף לאַנגע שוואַרצע שטראַלן.
אַ רעקלאַמע שניַדט זיך איִן אין הימל ווי אַ שווערד.
און שטימען שאַרכן, קושן זיך, אי יאָ אי ניט דערהערט,
און וויקלען זיך אַרויף ווי ליכטיקע ספּיראַלן.
און אויגן זוכן, אויגן זינגען, לאַכן.
אָבער מיר דאַכט, עס איז אַ טרויערן, עס איז דאָס לעצטע וואַכן,
די לעצטע שעה פֿון געזעגענען מיט דער ערד.

BROADWAY EVENING

Evening blossoms. The street rushes bright as a thousand springs.

Fires float up from the sundust and coral.

Shop windows—flaming caverns, waterfalls

of densest velvet, silk heavy and cool.

And people in an unending quadrille

meet each other and disappear.

Eyes searching, eyes singing, laughing,

but to me it seems all things are kneeling.

Blue shadows fall. The wind blossoms blue.

A car rushes by in long black streaks.

A billboard cuts into the sky like a sword.

Voices rustle, kiss, either heard or not

and spin upward like bright spirals.

Eyes searching, eyes singing, laughing.

But for me it is a grieving, it is the last watch,

the last hour of parting from the earth.

איך גיי דורך טױזט הױך-געװעלבטע טױערן,

װאָס הילכן אָפּ מיט פֿײערלעכער בראַנדז.

די זון שפּרייט זיך װי פֿון אָרגל אַ געזאַנג

דורך די צעפֿראַלטע גליענדיקע טױערן

מיט זייער טיף-געקריצטע עפֿאָפּעע

פֿון ליבע און פֿאַרצװייפֿלונג און רעװאָלט

און אַלץ, װאָס איז ניט געשען,

און האָב פֿלאַמענדיק געװאָלט.

און עטלעכע לאַנג דורכגעלעבטע שעהען אין די נישן —

סטאַטוען נאָקעטע, און אייביק יונג און שלאַנק.

אַ, גוט, ס'איז גוט דער װעג צו שרעק און אונטערגאַנג

דורך זון-פֿאַרשטראָאַמטע, זינגענדיקע טױערן.

GATES

I pass through a thousand high-vaulted gates

that resound with solemn bronze.

The sun spreads out like an organ's song

through the glowing gates flung open,

with their engraved epics

of love and despair and revolt,

everything that never happened

and yet was so passionately desired.

And several long-lived hours in the niches—

with nude statues, forever young and slender.

Yes, the road to fear and doom is pleasant

through singing gates, streaming with sunshine.

דורך בונטע שויבן

דורך בונטע הויכע שמאָלע שויבן
דערשווימט צו מיר דאָס גרויע לעבן.

איז יעדער מענטש אַ שלאָנקער פֿייער,
אַ וואָלקן, אַ טורעם, אַ חלום אַ נייער.

גייט יעדער אויף גאָלדענע, פורפורנע וועגן
גרויס און שווייגנדיק דעם טויט אַנטקעגן.

און די גאַנצע ערד איז אַ פֿאַרגייענדע זון,
אַ ריזיקע, פֿלאַמיקע, שטאַרבנדע בלום.

וואָס שיקט איר צאַנקענדן רעגן-בויגן
צו מיר דורך די הויכע בונטע שויבן.

160

THROUGH COLOURED PANES

Through tall, narrow, coloured panes
grey life wafts towards me.

Every person is a slender fire,
a cloud, a tower, a dream that's new.

Each one travels golden, crimson roads,
vast and silent, towards death.

And the entire earth is a setting sun,
a gigantic, flaming, dying flower

that sends her flickering rainbow
to me through tall, coloured panes.

דאָס שטאָלצע ליד

אויף גאָלדענע שטולן

אין הויכע פּאַלאַצן

זיצן די קעניגינס פֿון לעבן.

זייערע אויגן זײַנען האַרטע בריליאַנטן.

זייערע ליפֿן זײַנען רײַפֿע גראַנאַטן.

און מיט װײסע איידעלע הענט

טיילן זיי צװישן מענער

בעכערס מיט גיפֿט און בעכערס מיט גליק.

אויפֿן פֿינפֿטן שטאָק

אויף אַ צעבראָכענעם שטול

זיץ איך, די קעניגין פֿון װאָרט.

און מיט װײסע איידעלע פֿינגער

שאַף איך אַ ראָסע פֿון מענער,

פֿון פֿרױען און פֿאַרטראַכטע קינדער,

און טייל צװישן זיי

בעכערס מיט גיפֿט און בעכערס מיט גליק.

162

THE PROUD SONG

On golden thrones

in lofty palaces

sit the queens of life.

Their eyes hard diamonds.

Their lips ripe pomegranates.

With delicate white hands

they deal out among men

goblets of poison and goblets of joy.

On the fifth floor

on a broken throne

I sit, the queen of words.

And with delicate white hands

I create a race of men

and women and pensive children,

and deal out to them

goblets of poison and goblets of joy.

דער מאַסקאַראַד איז אויס

אויך איך האָב אין וואָלקנס געזען טיטאַנען.
עלפֿן האָבן געבלאָנדזשעט איבערן אַספֿאַלט.
שטערן האָבן געבליט אויף שטאָלענע שטאַמען
און הויך האָט געפֿלאַטערט דער אַלט
פֿון דעם טונקעלן קוסט.
די נאַכט, אַ יונגער נעגער מיט אַ רויז,
האָט לאַכנדיק געניגט זיך איבער מיר.

‫‪—‬‬ איך בין איצט אַלט
דער מאַסקאַראַד איז אויס.

און איך ליג בײַ די וואָרצלען פֿון זאַכן.
שווער יאָגט זייער פּולס דורך מײַן שטיינענדיק האַרץ.
עס איז אַ יערן, אַ וואַקסן, אַ טומלדיק וואַכן,
אַ פֿײַנלעך קלעטערן צום ליכט דורך שטיין און אַרץ.
די ערד קרײַזט פֿײַערלעך מיט אַלע אירע טויטע,
מיט קראַנקע טרוימענדיקע שטעט,
מיט באַרג און וואַלד און בליַיכן
שימערנדיקן גאָרטל פֿון וואַסערן.
און איבער איר די פֿײַערדיקע אומבאַקאַנטע צייכנס
פֿון שטערן, זונפֿאַרגאַנגען, מאָרגנרויטן.
געשטאַלטלאָז שפּרייטן זיך די נעכט און זינען אָן פֿאַרגלײַכן.
די שרעק פֿון טויט שרײַט פֿון אַלע טיפֿן,
און מילד לייגט זיך איבער זיי דאָס גאָלד פֿון לידער, העלע מיפֿן.

164

THE MASQUERADE IS OVER

I too have seen titans in the clouds.

Elves wandering over the asphalt.

Stars blooming on steel trunks

and an alto trilling loudly

from behind a dark bush.

Tonight, a young black with a rose

bent over me, laughing.

Now I am old—

the masquerade is over.

I lie at the root of things.

Their pulse rushes heavily through my wondering heart.

It is a ferment, a growth, a noisy vigil,

an anguished climb to light through stone and dross.

The earth circles solemnly with all its dead,

with diseased, dreamy cities,

with mountains and forests and pale

shimmering belts of water.

And over it the solemn, obscure markings

of stars, sunsets, red dawns.

The nights extend, shapeless, incomparable.

The fear of death shrieks from the depths,

gently laying over them the gold of poems, bright myths.

און אַלע לעבנס זײַנען רײַך אין טרויער און זײַנען ענלעך,

און גרויס איז אַלץ און אומפֿאַרשטענדלעך.

All lives are rich in sorrow and are alike,

and everything is immense and incomprehensible.

ראובן לודוויג

אַ שווערער טאָג צווישן קבֿרים.

דער הימל איז בלײַערן, דער הימל איז גרוי.

איך וועל גיין אין גאַס און אפֿשר טרעפֿן

לודוויגן מיט זײַן שיינער פֿרוי.

ער וועט טראָגן דעם מאַנטל איבערן אָרעם,

מיר וועלן גיין צווישן לידער, ווי צווישן טאָפּאָלן,

און ער וועט פֿרעגן לאַשטשענדיק, אײַנפֿאַך אַזוי:

"איז וואָס זשע מאַכט איר, מאַרגאַלין?"

מיט רייד פֿאַרנאַכטיקע שטילע

דערמאָנען מיר אים,

מיט רייד ווי אַ טרער, ווי אַ תּפֿילה,

ווי דער אָנריר פֿון ליבע פֿינגער

און דינע,

פֿאַרנאַכטיקע, שטילע...

ער איז געווען אַ לירישער ציגײַנער, אַ מענטש פֿון דרום,

שטורעמדיק, שטאָלץ און ריטערלעך-גוט.

ער פֿלעגט טראָגן דעם מאַנטל איבערן אָרעם,

מיט ברייטע ראַנדן דעם הוט.

REUBEN LUDWIG*

A hard day among the graves.

The sky is leaden, the sky is grey.

I will go into the street, perhaps, meet

Ludwig with his pretty wife.

He will carry his coat over his arm,

we will stroll among poems as among poplars,

and flatteringly, he will inquire, so simply:

"So, how are you, Margolin?"

With quiet, dusky talk

we remember him,

with words like a teardrop, like a prayer,

like the touch of beloved fingers

and slender,

dusky, quiet. . .

He was a lyrical gypsy, a man from the south,

stormy, proud, and chivalrous.

He used to carry his cloak over his arm,

his hat with the wide brim.

* Ludwig, Reuben (1895–1936) Yiddish poet born in the Ukraine, emigrated to New York at age fifteen. One of the *In-Zikh* group of Yiddish poets. He sympathized with and wrote of various ethnic minorities including Negroes.

מיר פֿלעגן גיין צווישן לידער, ווי צווישן טאָפֿאָלן...

און זײַן קול, האַסטיק און בריט,

האָט געמישט אומגעניט ווי אין אַ טיגל

רויטע ערד, וואָלקנס, פֿאַרלאָשענע פֿרייד,

די מיסיסיפּי, און שבֿטים, און טאָלן.

ער איז ניט געוואָרן קיין ציטערדיקע פּלייט,

ניט קיין מלאך מיט אײדעלע פֿליגל,

ניט קיין איינער פֿון די אָפּליאָקירטע סימבאָלן.

ער איז געוואָרן אַ מענטש אַ פּשוטער, הייס און באַטריבט,

און אַזאַ האָבן מיר אים געליבט.

און געדענקען וועלן מיר די שוואָרצהויטיקע שלעגער,

די באַרגיקע ליפֿן פֿון נעגער,

דייזי מעקלעלאָן, די אומפֿרוכטבאַרע מוטער,

אפֿשר דאָס אַלץ, אפֿשר ניט מער.

ווײַל לודוויג, דער צו יונג מידער,

איז שענער געוואָרן פֿאַר זײַנע לידער.

מיר וועלן גיין צווישן לידער, ווי צווישן טאָפֿאָלן.

ער וועט פֿרעגן לאַשטשענדיק, איינפֿאַך אַזוי:

"איז וואָס זשע מאַכט איר, מאַרגאָלין?"

170

We used to stroll among poems, as among poplars. . .

And his voice, impetuous, far-reaching,
ineptly mixed as in a melting-pot
red earth, clouds, extinguished joy,
the Mississippi, and tribes and valleys.
He was not a trembling flute,
nor an angel with delicate wings,
nor one of those faded symbols.

He was a plain person, hot and sad,
and as such we loved him.

We will remember the swarthy fighters,
the mountainous lips of the black
Daisy McClellan, the barren mother,
perhaps that is all, perhaps no more.
Because Ludwig, that too soon weary one,
was handsomer than any of his poems.

We will stroll among the poems as among poplars.
And flatteringly he will inquire, so simply:
"So, how are you, Margolin?"

טויט-מיד פֿון דער לאַסט פֿון אַ חלום

"װעלט" שרײַבן מיר אין זאַמד

און "גאָט".

און טויט-מיד פֿון דער לאַסט פֿון אַ חלום,

און אַ ביסל מיט שפּאָט

קריצן מיר טיף אײַן אין זאַמד"

"אײביקייט".

און עס גייט שווער און בלינד אונדזער האַנט,

װי דורך אַ שטורעם.

עפּעס װעט מוזן, מוזן בלײַבן אויף דער ערד:

אַ גלאַנץ פֿון קיינעם ניט געזען,

אַ וואָרט פֿון קיינעם ניט געהערט.

172

DEAD TIRED FROM THE BURDEN OF A DREAM

"World" we inscribed in the sand,

and "God".

And dead tired from the burden of a dream,

and with a little mockery

deep into the sand we carved:

"Eternity".

Our hands moved heavily and blindly,

as through a storm.

Something must remain upon the earth:

an unseen radiance,

an unheard word.

בלויז איין ליד

איך האָב בלויז איין ליד —
פֿון ייִאוש און שטאָלץ.
עס טונקלט און גליט
אין בראָנדז און שטאָל.

אַ רויִער אַקאָרד.
פֿיל שוווייגן, פֿיל שאָטן.
איך פֿורעם דאָס וואָרט
מיט מײַן לעצטן אָטעם.

מיט זכרונות שווער,
ווידער און ווידער
גיי איך ווי אַ שווערד
דורך די לידער.

174

JUST ONE POEM

I have but one poem—

of despair and pride.

It darkens and glows

in bronze and in steel.

A crude chord.

Much silence, much shadow.

I shape the word

with my last breath.

Again and again,

with heavy memories,

I go through the poems

like a sword.

צו פֿראַנץ ווערפֿעל

"ווי זעליג זינד וויר,
די אין פֿאַרמען וואָהנען".
פֿראַנץ ווערפֿעל

אַזוי איז עס שטענדיק געווען:
בין געוואַקסן צווישן זײַלן פֿון לידער.
גרויסער ברודער, עס איז ניט קיין גליק, ניין.
מײַנע פֿליגל האָבן צו הויך מיך דערהויבן
איבער מענטשן, איבערן לעבן.
אין לערן רוים בין איך אַ טרויעריקע סטאַטוע,
אַ זינגענדיקער שטיין.
ווי פֿון אַ פֿײַנדלעכן שטערן
שווימען שטימען, געלעכטער, געוויין.
גאָט, איך בין צו פֿיל אַליין.

176

TO FRANZ WERFEL*

> "How blissful we are
> Who live in forms."
>   Franz Werfel

That's how it always was:

growing among the columns of poetry.

Big brother, it was no pleasure, no.

My wings lifted me too high

above people, above life.

I am a grieving statue in empty space,

a singing stone

as from a hostile star.

Voices, laughter and lament float up.

God, I am alone too much.

* Werfel, Franz (1890–1945) Austrian novelist, poet and playwright. Born in Prague, he fled Nazi Germany in 1938 and immigrated to the United States where he died in California.

מיר וועלן בויען א וואנט*

מיר וועלן בויען אַ וואַנט,

אַז דאָס טרומייטן

וועגן די נײַע צײַטן,

אַז דער געפילדדער

וועגן דער גרויסשטאַט דער ווילדער,

און די געשרייען

וועגן משיחישע ווייען

אויפֿן בראָקשטול פֿון פֿאַרלאָרענע וועלטן

און דערגלײַכן

זאָל צו אונדז דאָ ניט דערגרייכן.

שמייכלענדיק בויען אַ וואַנט.

אונדז וועט פֿאַרבליבן די שטילקייט — דאָס האַרץ פֿון דעם שטורעם,

אַ וועלט וואָס איז פֿראָסט און דערהויבן און אָרעם.

דער בליק, און דער זשעסט, און געפֿליסטער פֿון ליבע און שטאַרבנדע זאַכן,

פֿון פֿילפֿאַכן ריטעם פֿון לעבן די פֿאַרהוילענע גרונט-מעלאָדי.

און אפֿשר וועלן מיר נאָך יאָרן מי

אײַנקריצן אין לבֿנה-שײַן פֿון דורכזיכטיקע שורות

דעם לײַכסטן בייג פֿון אַ צווײַג,

*די ערשטע העלפֿט פֿון ר. אײַזלאַנד.

178

* WE WILL BUILD A WALL

We will build a wall

so that the trumpeting

about new times,

so that the racket

about the wild metropolis

and the clamour

about the pangs of the Messiah

on the birthing stool of lost worlds

and all that

will not intrude on us.

With a smile, build a wall.

For us the silence will remain—the eye of the storm,

a world that is crass, exalted and poor.

The glance, the gesture, the whispers from love and from dying things

from the complex rhythms concealed in the melody of life.

Perhaps, after years of toil, we will

engrave with transparent lines

the lightest arc of a bough in the moonlight,

like little black birds in flight,

* The first half is by Reuben Ayzland (Margolin's companion)

179

ווי שוואַרצע טאַנצנדיקע שטערן

קלײנע פֿײגל אין פֿלי,

דאָס קול פֿון צער טיף קלינגענדיק און גרוי,

די בלײכע לײכטנדיקע ליפֿן פֿון אַ מידער פֿרוי.

the black and dancing stars

the grey sound of sorrow emerges from the depths

on the pale luminous lips of a weary woman.

MARY

מאַרי

Mari

וואָס ווילסטו, מאַרי?

וואָס ווילסטו, מאַרי?

אפֿשר אַ קינד זאָל ליכטיק דרימלען אין מײַן שויס.
די טיפֿע שטומע אָוונטן אין שטערענגן הויז
אַליין, פֿאַמעלעך וואַנדערנדיק.
אַלץ וואַרטנדיק און וואַרטנדיק.
און זאָל מײַן ליבע זײַן צום מאַן, וואָס ליבט מיך ניט,
שטיל און ווי פֿאַרצווייפֿלונג גרויס.

וואָס ווילסטו, מאַרי?

איך וואָלט געוואָלט די פֿיס פֿאַרוואָרצלט אין דער ערד,
אַליין שטיין אין דער מיט פֿון טויַיק-העלן פֿעלד.
עס גייט די זון דורך מיר ווי דורך אַ יונגער וועלט,
דאָס רײצפֿן און דער דופֿט פֿון דרימלענדיקן פֿעלד.
און פלוצעם יאָגט זיך אַן אַ ברייטער ווילדער רעגן
און שלאָגט און קושט מיך טומלדיק און שווער,
אַ שטורעם ווי אַן אָדלער קומט געפֿלויגן,
זינקט שרײצענדיק אין מיר און בייגט מיך הין און הער.

184

WHAT DO YOU WANT, MARY?

What do you want, Mary?

Perhaps a child brightly drowsing in my lap.
Deeply silent evenings in the stern house
alone, wandering slowly.
Constantly waiting, waiting.
May my love be for him who loves me not,
quiet and like despair, immense.

What do you want, Mary?

I want my feet rooted in the earth,
want to stand alone in the midst of a dew-bright field.
The sun going through me as through a young world,
the ripeness and fragrance of that dreamy field.
Suddenly a broad and savage rain beats down,
drenches me, kisses me tumultuously and hard,
a storm flies at me like an eagle,
sinks screeching into me, bending me this way and that.

בין איך אַ מענטש, אַ בליץ, דער אומרו פֿון די וועגן,

אָדער די שוואַרצע קרעכצנדיקע ערד?

איך וייס ניט מער. מיט טרערן-שווערע אויגן

גיב איך זיך אָפ דער זון, דעם ווינט און רעגן.

אָבער וואָס ווילסטו, מאַרי?

Am I a person, a spark, the mischief of the roads,

or the black, moaning earth?

I no longer know. With tearful eyes

I give myself up to the sun, the wind, the rain.

But what do you want, Mary?

גאָט, הכנענעהדיק און שטום זײַנען די וועגן.

דורכן פֿײַער פֿון זינד און פֿון טרערן

פֿירן צו דיר אַלע וועגן.

איך האָב פֿון ליבע געבויט דיר אַ נעסט

און פֿון שטילקייט אַ טעמפּל.

איך בין דײַן היטערין, דינסט און געליבטע,

און דײַן פּנים האָב איך קיין מאָל ניט געזען.

און איך ליג אויפֿן ראַנד פֿון דער וועלט,

און דו גייסט פֿינצטער דורך מיר ווי די שעה פֿון טויט,

גייסט ווי אַ ברייטע בליצנדיקע שווערד.

MARY'S PRAYER

God, meek and silent are the ways.

Through the flames of sin and tears

all roads lead to You.

I built You a nest of love

and from silence, a temple.

I am Your guardian, servant and lover,

yet I have never seen Your face.

I lie at the edge of the world,

while You pass through me darkly like the hour of death,

You pass like a broad, flashing sword.

מאַרי און דער פּריסטער

מאַרי, ביסט אַ בעכער מיט אָפּפֿערװײַן,

אַ צאַרט פֿאַררונדיקטער בעכער מיט װײַן

אױף אַ פֿאַרװײַסטן מזבח.

אַ פּריסטער

מיט שלאַנקע לאַנגזאַמע הענט

הײבט אױף הױך דעם קרישטאָלענעם בעכער.

און עס ציטערט דײַן לעבן און ברענט

אין זײַנע אױגן, אין זײַנע הענט

און װײַל אין גליק עקסטאַטישן און שװערן

צעשמעטערט װערן.

מאַרי. מאַרי,

באַלד װעט מיט אַ העל געװײַן

דײַן לעבן זיך צעברעכן,

און פֿאַרבן װעט דײַן טױט

דעם טױטן שטײן

הײס און רױט.

און עס װעלן שמײכלען די פֿאַרגעסענע געטער

הײס און רױט.

MARY AND THE PRIEST

Mary, you are a goblet of Ophir wine,

a delicately rounded goblet of wine

on a sacrificial altar.

A priest

with delicate, cautious hands,

raises the crystal goblet high.

Your life trembles and burns

in his eyes, in his hands,

and wants to be crushed

in profound ecstatic joy.

Mary, Mary,

soon your life will shatter

with a light lament,

and your death will be painted

on dead stone,

hot and red.

And forgotten gods will smile

hot and red.

צװישן מענטשן איז זי
װי אין מידבר געװען,
פֿלעגט זי מורמלען אַלײן
איר נאָמען: ‏‏"מאַרי‏".

און געװעזן מאַרי
און אױך געליבטער מאַן:
‏"װי דורך הײסן טומאַן,
מאַרי,
הער איך דײַן קול,
זע איך דײַן שאָטן‏",
פֿלעגט זי מורמלען אַ מאָל
אונטער איר אָטעם.

און בלעטערן װײיך
דאָס גליק דאָס אַרױסגעטראַכטע,
און װערן פּלוצעם בלײיך
פֿון זעלבסטפֿאַראַכטונג.

LONELY MARY

She is with people
as if in the desert,
murmuring her name
to herself: Mary.

And there was Mary
and also her beloved man:
"Mary,
as through a hot mist,
I hear your voice
and see your shadow,"
she would sometimes murmur
under her breath.

Softly leafing
through imagined joy,
and paling suddenly
from self–contempt.

מאַרי גייט איבער די צימערן אויף און אָפּ,
צעשטעלט די פֿרוכט, דעם ווײַן, די שלאַנקע בלומען,
נייגט זיך, שמייכלט אין פֿאַרווירטער לוסט,
און די שטוב איז פּוסט,
כאָטש אַלע זײַנען זיי געקומען.

זאָל איצט איר אַרן, וואָס אַ יוגנט לאַנג
האָט זי געצאַנקט אין אַט דעם אַלטנס זונפֿאַרגאַנג?
זאָל אַרן איר, וואָס האָט פֿאַרכאַפּט אַ מאָל איר אָטעם
דאָס טרויערשפּיל פֿון לעבן, ווען עס לעשט זיך,
באַגלייט פֿון ייִאוש און פֿון בלענדנדן געדאַנק?
געוועזן איז ער לאַנג דערנאָך דער גרויסער שאַטן
איבער זיי אַלעמען, טרוימער, האַרן, קנעכט,
וועמען זי האָט געקענט אין די נעכט.
דו שווייגנדיקער, ייִנגל ברוינער,
פֿרעמדער, ווי פֿאַרבלאָנדזשעט פֿון אַ שטערן,
ביסט געווען מײַן נאַכט אין ווײַסן צימער, אין אַ פֿרילינג
און מיסטיש טונקלער ווײַן אין הויכן בעכער.
און דו האַלב הייליקער און האַלב פֿאַרברעכער,
צי גאָר פֿאַעט. געדענקסט די שאַרפֿע פֿרייד,
די אויסברוכן פֿון צערטלעכקייט און צאָרן
און צו לעצט דאָס מערכענהאָפֿטע פֿאָרן
דורך זומער און דורך דרימלענדיקע שטעט?

194

MARY AND THE GUESTS

Mary goes from room to room, in and out,

arranges the fruit, the wine, the slender flowers,

bows, smiles in agitated joy,

the house is empty,

though everyone came.

Should she now mind that long ago when young

she had flickered in this old man's sunset?

Should she care, who once had caught her breath

at the sad game of an ebbing life

attended by despair and blinding thoughts?

Long afterwards, he remained the great shadow

over all of them—dreamers, lords and slaves,

whom she knew in the nights.

You, silent brown youth,

strayed from a star, like an alien,

you were my night in the white room one springtime

and also the mystic dark wine in tall goblets.

And you, half-holy, half-criminal,

or altogether a poet. Remember that sharp joy,

the outbursts of tenderness and fury

and at the end, the fateful journey

through summer and through dreamy cities?

און דו, און דו, און דו — אַ לאַנגע קייט.

און דאָס קינד איז דאָ.

עס איז געקומען צו דער מוטערס טיר פֿון זייער ווײַט.

עס האָט אין ווינקל זיך פֿאַרדרוקט, קליין און פֿול מיט טרויעריקייט.

עס איז אין זיך פֿאַרטיפֿט, דאָס קינד, און שטיל און ווײַס.

אויגן, קלאָגט מיך ניט אָן, אויגן קערט זיך ניט אָפּ.

בעטלער, זײַ געגריסט! ביסט מיאוס און פֿינצטער ווי אַ ראָב,

דאָך האָב איך געזען דיך ליכטיק לאָכן ווי אַ גאָט

איין מאָל אין שניי און שטורעם.

און אָט איז אַ גרינער שטערן, צוויי קוסטעס פֿון יאַסמין,

אַ ברונעם אין אַ הויף — אַלץ געסט פֿון ליטע.

און אַ חתונה, צעבליטע לוסט, און מענטשן קעפּ אויף קעפּ,

און גאַסן אין ווירוואַר, און פֿײַערן לאַנג פֿאַרגליטע.

און אַ ריז אַן אולם צווישן מויערן אָנגעקלעמט.

און אויסגעהאָקט פֿון ווילדסטן חלום —

שווינדלדלדיקע ווינדלטרעפּ.

אין טרויער פֿון די נעכט, אין אַ ווײַטער שטאָט,

פֿלעגן זיי אויפֿשטײַגן פֿון בענקנדיקן בלוט

און פֿלעגן פֿירן זי אַרויף, אַרויף —

ווּהין?

אפֿשר גאָר אין יענער נידעריקער שטוב,

וווּ נעפּלדיק, נאָענט

בלײַכן זיך בײַם לאָמפּ

דער מוטערס גרויער קאָפּ,

196

You, and you, and you—a long chain.

And the child is here.

It arrived at mother's door from a great distance.

Crawled into a corner, small, suffused with sadness.

This child, sunken into itself, silent and pale.

Eyes, don't reproach me, eyes, don't turn away.

Greetings, beggar! You are ugly and black as a raven,

yet once in a snowstorm

I saw you laughing brightly like a god.

Here are a green star, two bushes of jasmine,

a well in the yard—the guests from Lithuania.

A wedding, full of people, bubbling with joy,

streets in confusion, fires long since banked

An immense crowd clamped between walls.

And carved out of the wildest dream—

dizzying, winding stairs.

In a distant city, in nightly sorrow

they would arise with yearning blood

and would carry her aloft, aloft—

Whereto?

Perhaps even into that humble house

nearby, where hazily,

mother's grey head,

mother's quiet hands

דער מוטערס שטילע הענט.

אויגן, קלאָגט מיך ניט אָן, אויגן, קערט זיך ניט אָפ.

אַ פליסטערן, אַ שאַרכן, שטילער שפּאַט.

מאַרי איבער די צימערן גייט אויף און אָפּ.

עס איז אָראָפ אויף איר אַ קאַלטע רו.

אַלץ ווייטער, אומבאַקאַנטער ווערן איר די געסט.

ווער ביסטו דו? און דו ווער ביסט? און דו?

זי איז אַליין. ביי אַ פרעמדן פֿעסט.

זי איז קיין מאָל ניט געווען מיט זיי פֿאַרוועבט.

זי האָט איר לעבן קיין מאָל ניט געלעבט.

198

fade in the lamplight.

Eyes, don't reproach me, eyes, don't turn away.

A whisper, a rustle, quiet mocking.

Mary goes from room to room, in and out.

A chilly calm descends upon her.

Her guests are more distant, more unfamiliar.

Who are you? And who are you? And you?

She is alone. At someone else's celebration.

She was never part of it.

She never lived her own life.

מאַרי וויל זײַן אַ בעטלעריין

זײַן אַ בעטלעריין.

ווי פֿון אַ שיף, וואָס זינקט,

וואַרפֿן אַלע אוצרות אויפֿן ווינט:

די לאַסט פֿון דײַן ליבע און לאַסט פֿון די פֿריידן,

און אַז איר אַליין זאָל מער זיך ניט דערקאָנען —

אויך מײַן גוטן צי מײַן שלעכטן נאָמען.

זײַן אַ בעטלעריין.

שטום זיך שאַרן איבער גרויע טראָטואַרן,

ווי דער שוואַרצער שאָטן פֿון אַלע העלע לעבנס,

און פֿאַר געשאָנקטע גראָשנס

קויפֿן זיך צום שפּילן

אַ וואָנזיניקן חלום און אַ שטילן,

וואָס קנוילט זיך זילבעריק אין רויך פֿון אָפּיום.

אײַנשלאָפֿן אין גאַס אונטער דער זון,

ווי אין פֿעלד אַ מידער זאַנג,

ווי אַ צעפֿליקטע בלום,

וואָס איז פֿאַרוועלקט און אומריין,

און דאָך געטלעך,

און האָט נאָך אַלץ אַ פֿאַר שיינע זײַדענע בלעטלעך.

און אויפֿלײַכטן מיט קראַנקן ליכט פֿון אַ לאַמטערן,

זיך אויסוויקלען פֿון דער שטומער גרויער נאַכט,

ווי אַ נעפֿל פֿון נעפֿל, ווי אַ נאַכט פֿון דער נאַכט.

200

MARY WANTS TO BE A BEGGAR WOMAN

To be a beggar woman.

To throw all treasures to the wind,

as from a sinking ship—

the burden of your love, the burden of happiness—

so that I could no longer recognize

my good or my bad name.

To be a beggar woman.

To shuffle mutely over grey sidewalks

like the dark shadow of all bright lives,

and with the pennies I am given

buy myself a crazy, quiet dream

to play with,

which curls silvery in the smoke of opium.

To fall asleep in the street under the sun

like a weary stalk in the fields,

like a tattered flower

that is withered and unclean

and yet, Godlike,

still retains a few silken petals.

To flare up in the sickly light of a lantern,

to unwrap myself from the silent, grey night,

like fog upon fog, like night upon night.

ווערן אַ געבעט און ווערן אַ פֿלאַם.

זיך אַוועקשעענקען צערטלעך, ברענענדיק און גרויזאַם.

און זײַן אײַנזאַם,

ווי נאָר קעניגן און בעטלערס זײַנען אײַנזאַם.

און אומגליקלעך.

און גיין אַזוי מיט פֿאַרוווּנדערטע אויגן

דורך גרויסע סודותדיקע טעג און נעכט

צום הויכן געריכט,

צום שמערצלעכן ליכט,

צו זיך.

Become a prayer, become a flame.

To give myself away, tender, burning, cruel.

And be alone,

as only kings and beggars are alone.

And unhappy.

And walk thus, with wondering eyes

through great, mysterious days and nights

toward the high court,

toward the painful light,

toward myself.

מאַרי און דער טויט

ס'האָט מאַרי זיך געזעגנט מיטן ליכטיקן הויז,
פֿאַר די וועגט זיך געניגט און געניגט און אַרויס.

און אַוועק אין דער נאַכט, ווי מען גייט אין אַ וואַלד,
ווּ גאָטס אָטעם איז נאָענט און ס'שרעקט יעדע געשטאַלט.

די נאַכט האָט געלייגט זיך ווייך אויף איר ווײ,
געלייגט זיך ווי שוואַרצער, ווי לאַשטשענדער שניי.

און געגאַנגען נאָך איר זיינען פֿריילעך און בונט
בעטלער און שיכּור און וואַגאַבונד.

ווי טרויעריקע פֿייגל, קראַנק פֿאַרליבט,
האָבן קאַליקעס נאָכגעהיפט.

און קרעציקע האָבן פֿאַרשעמטע גענענט
און זיך די ווּנדן פֿאַרשטעלט מיט די הענט.

און פֿאָרויס איז געגאַנגען פֿאַרבענקטערהייט
דער יינגלינג טויט מיט דער טונקעלער פֿלייט.

204

MARY AND DEATH

Mary said goodbye to the bright house,
nodded to the walls, bowed, and left.

Departed in the night, as into a forest,
where God's breath is near and every shape is feared.

The night lay gently on her pain,
lay like black, caressing snow.

And following her happily and jauntily—
beggar and drunkard and vagabond.

Cripples hobbled along behind
like sorrowful birds sick with love.

And the mangy ones drew near, shamefaced,
covering their wounds with their hands.

And out in front, full of yearning,
went death, the youth with a dark flute.

IMAGES

געששטאַלטן

Geshtaltn

_____

ער האָט געוווּסט:

ער איז אַ ניט-פֿאַרענדיקטער עקספּערימענט

אין גרויסע לײַדנשאַפֿטן, אמת, פּאַזע,

אַ ניט-דערבאַקענע מעטאַמאָרפֿאָזע

פֿון הויכן גלוטיקן געדאַנק

אין אָרעם פֿלייש און בלוט,

מיט מיליאָנען אַנדערע האַלב-ריזן און האַלב-גנאָמען

אַ שפּאַטישער אומניצלעכער באַוווּיז,

אַז דער אַלמעכטיקער קען שוואַך

זײַן פֿאָך.

אָפֿט מאָל פֿלעגט ער טראַכטן, שפּאַנענדיק אין שטוב:

"כּדי אַ באַרג זאָל זײַן, מוז דען זײַן אַ גרוב?"

"נו, גאָט, איך וועל דערשלעפּן ווי ניט איז דעם עול".

און ער פֿלעגט שמייכלען מיד און איבערקלוג,

גלעטן זיך דעם פּליך, רייכערן פֿאָל-מאָל,

זען ווי איבער טרעפּ פֿון יאָדע, אַמעטיסט

פֿאַמעלעך קײַקלען זיך די טעג.

און זיך אַליין אַ מאָל פֿאַרטרויען ווי אַ סוד:

"ווי איך בין אַ ייִד...

208

A HUMAN BEING

He knew

with a real though affected passion,

he was not a completed experiment

a half-baked metamorphosis

of elevated glowing thoughts

and paltry flesh and blood,

along with millions of other

half giants and half gnomes,

mocking and needless proof

that the Almighty barely knew

His trade.

Sometimes, pacing the house, he would speculate:

"Can you have a mountain without having a pit?"

"Well, fine, I'll bear it as if it weren't a burden".

And he would smile wearily, too clever by half,

smoothing his bald pate, smoking Pall Malls,

watching jade and amethyst

spill over the steps

as the days slowly unfolded.

And sometimes, would tell himself in secret:

"As I am a Jew. . .

ווי איך בין אַ ייִד'',

עס איז ניט די קלענסטע צווישן העלדישקייטן

טרינקען שוואַרצע קאַווע

אין אַן אויגנבליק,

וואָס העכגט אומזיכער צווישן אייביקייטן,

און אויפֿהייבן די קאַווע פֿאַר אַ טאָסט''

‏‏''גאָט, איך בעט דיר מוחל, הערסט?

איך בין דיר מוחל, גאָט''.

as I am a Jew . . ."

It isn't the smallest of heroics

to drink black coffee

in the blink of an eye

that hangs uncertainly between eternities,

and raise the coffee in a toast.

"God, I forgive You, You hear?

I forgive You, God".

ס'האָבן שטיינער געלייגט זיך ווי גראָז און ווי טוי

אונטערן צעפֿליקטן שלעפּ פֿון דער פֿרוי,

וואָס איז געגאַנגען לאַכנדיק אין רעגן

און הויך אויפֿגעריכט.

קינדער זיינען אָנגעלאָפֿן אומגעריכט,

געשפּריצט אַרום איר מיט אַ סווישטשען און קרייען,

און געטראַכט האָט זי, אַז משוגע

זיינען זייערע געשרייען.

און ווי פֿייגלכאַרן

האָבן זיי זיך אויפֿגעלייזט און זיך פֿאַרלאָרן

אין אויסגעטרוימטער דרימלענדער מוזיק.

און ס'איז אַלץ וואָס געוועזן, געקומען צוריק.

געקומען מיט גוטסקייט.

געבעטן פֿאַרגעבן

פֿאַרן צער, וואָס האָט אַ מאָל געגעבן.

אויף אַ ווײַלע האָט איר פּנים זיך פֿאַרטונקלט

און ווי אַ מאָל זיך געקאָרטשעט פֿון שאַנד,

און זי האָט אַ ווײַלע געצעגערט

און באַלד מיט אַ ברייטן פֿיר פֿון דער האַנט

אַלצדינג, אַלצדינג פֿאַרגעבן.

זיינען שטימען זינגענדיק פֿאַרבײַגעפֿלויגן,

האָט אַ באַקאַנט הויז אויף דער עלפֿט זיך פֿאַרבײַגן

און טריב געשאַרט זיך צו איר מיטן הילצערנעם שוועל,

THE MADWOMAN

Stones were laid like grass and dew

under the woman's ragged hem,

as laughing and highly excited

she went out into the rain.

Children came running unexpectedly,

stalking her, whistling and crowing,

and she thought to herself

that their screaming was insane.

Like a chorus of birds

they dissolved and lost themselves in

imaginary, dreamy music.

And all that had been, returned,

returned with goodness.

Begged forgiveness

for inflicted sorrows of the past.

For a time, her face darkened

and as before, writhed in shame

she paused for a bit

but then with a generous wave of her hand,

she forgave it all, forgave everything.

Singing voices flew by,

a familiar house leaned over,

shuffled eagerly toward her with its wooden doorstep

וואָס זי פֿלעגט אַ מאָל, ווי אויף אַ באַפֿעל,

באַטרעטן מיט זינקנדע פֿיס.

און זי האָט זיך געוווּנדערט ווי נאָענט דאָס איז,

אַ גליק, ווי נאָענט עס טומלען די ליבע טריט;

און עמענצנס אויגן האָבן זיך פּלוצעם צעבליט,

זי פֿאַרבלענדט און פֿאַרווירט

און דאָס לײַב אירס באַריִרט.

און אַלץ רופֿנדער ברייטער גערוישט האָט מוזיק

אין דער לופֿטן

און ווי אַ שטורעם געצוקט דורך אירע אַקסלען און היפֿטן.

און פֿאַרהויבן דאָס קלייד אין די הענט,

דעם קאָפּ אויף צוריק,

אונטערן ליאַרעם פֿון קינדער

און יאָמערנדן רעגן

האָט זי פֿאַמעלעך, פֿיִערלעך אַנטקעגנגעטאַנצט

איר טויטן לעבן.

214

she would cross with sinking feet,

as if on command.

She wondered at how close it was,

oh, joy, how the beloved steps were rattling nearby;

someone's eyes suddenly blossomed,

dazzled and agitated her

and stirred her body.

The music became more insistent, rushing

through the air

like a storm quivering through her shoulders and hips.

She lifted her dress in her hands,

looked back,

and amid the clamour of children

and the lamenting rain,

slowly, solemnly, danced toward

her dead life.

אין טיר פֿון טענעממענט, ווו פֿון די טרעפּ אַראָפּ

רײסט אויף די פֿינצטערניש דאָס אויג פֿון אַ לאַמטערן,

שטײגט ווי אין הײליקן שײן זײן קאָפּ.

אויפֿן שטיינערנעם געזיכט די אויגן פֿון מעטאַל,

קײלעכדיק און ליכטיק, אָן ערינערונגען,

האָבן די גאַס מיט יעדן דורכגייער און יעדן אויטאָשטראַל

אין הונגעריקער לערקײט אײנגעשלונגען.

ער טוט אַ הייב דעם אַקסל לײכט און שאַרף,

אַ שאַר, אַ בײג, אין טאַש דעם סטילעט דעם קילן,

עס ליגט די גאַס פֿאַר אים ווי אַ גאָלדענע האַרף,

און זײנע ווילדע פֿינגער יאָגן זיך צום שפּילן.

THE GANGSTER

In the tenement doorway, down the steps,

the eye of a lamp rends the darkness,

his head rises as in a halo.

In his stony face the metallic eyes,

round and bright, devoid of memory.

Every passerby, every headlight in the street

swallowed up by the hungry void.

He shrugs, sharp and easy,

a shuffle, an arch, the cold stiletto in his pouch,

the street lies before him like a golden harp,

and his wild fingers rush to play.

אין טונקעלן צימער

אין טונקעלן צימער שטייען זאכן וואך ווי די הינט.

הערן ווידער דעם צאפל פֿון וואלד, די האק אין ווינט,

אַ וואָרט פֿאַרשטיקט צווישן וועגט, דעם זיפֿץ פֿון אַ קינד.

אומרויִקע באַלאַדן שפילט דער לאַמטערן-שטראַל

אויפֿן שוואַרצן מאַנסטער דעם ראַיאַל.

עס ברומט דאָס האָלץ.

עס טײטלט אַ פֿינגער און שווימט

איבערן פֿאַרהאַנגס פֿליגל

און פֿאַרבייגט זיך אין שפיגל.

און טרויער שוויומט פֿון די ווינקלען לבֿנהדיק-בלינד,

ציט אַרויף זיך פֿאַרעקשנט, פֿאַרבענקט, פֿאַרשפינט

אין אַ שווערן היאַצינט.

אַ האַנט אויפֿן פֿאַרהאַנג.

אַ שאָטן אין שײן.

די טונלעלע פֿרוי קומט אַרײן.

דעם פֿאַטעל שלינגט זי אײן, זי פֿאַרשווינדט.

זי איז בלויז אַ וואַזע פֿאַרן גרויסן טרויעריקן היאַצינט.

218

IN THE DARK ROOM

In the dark room objects stand watch like hounds.

Hear again the quiver of the forest, the chop of the wind,

a word repressed between walls, the sigh of a child.

The beam of the lamp plays restless ballads

on the monstrous black grand piano.

The wood hums.

A finger points and floats

over the curtain's wings,

and bends toward the mirror.

Sorrow wafts from the corners, moon-blind,

draws itself up stubbornly, yearningly,

spinning into a heady hyacinth.

A hand on the curtain.

A shadow in the light.

The dark woman enters.

The armchair swallows her up, she disappears.

She is only a vase for the great, sad hyacinth.

1

ווען איך זאָל זײַן אַ קעניגין
און וואָלסט מײַן פּאַזש געווען,
אַ ייִנגל פֿרוייענהאָפֿט און דין,
און פֿאַלש און שיין,

וואָלסטו דורך זילבערנע אַלייען
מײַן פערל אויסגעגנייטן טרעגן,
דו מיט מײַן מאַלפּע זאַלבעצוווייען,
געטראַגן צאַרנדיק און פֿאַרנעם.

און וואָלסטו געמוזט דאַן זײַן מײַן היטער,
ווען אין אַ בליציקן גאַלאָפּ
קומט ער, מײַן אָדלער און מײַן ריטער,
און איך דעם גאָלד באַשטויבטן קאָפּ

וואָלט צירלעך צו אים צוגעבויגן,
די שמאָלע ליפּן, ווײַך און רויט,
און דורך די האַלב פֿאַרמאַכטע אויגן
וואָלט איך געזען, ווי דער טויט

צוקט אין דײַן בליק דורך שאַרף און גרין,
אויף דײַנע ליפּן בלײַך ווי אַש,

THE GIRL DECLARES

1

If I were a queen
and you my page—
a youth, feminine and slender,
false but beautiful—

both you and my monkey
would stiffly and grandly carry
through silvery avenues
my pearl-embroidered train.

You must then be my protector,
when, at a lightning gallop
he arrives—my eagle and my knight—
and I would elegantly bend toward him

my gold-dusted head
my pursed lips, soft and red,
and through half-closed eyes
I would see how death

quivers in your glance, sharp and green
on your pale and ashen lips—

ווען איך וואָלט זײַן אַ קעניגין,

און דו מײַן פּאַזש.

2

דײַנע ווערטער זײַנען שטיינער.

דײַנע ווערטער זײַנען בײַטשן.

בלוט שטראָמט.

איך וועל צומאַכן די אויגן.

איך וועל זײַן באַלד אין אַ שטילן לאַנד.

איך וועל גיין אויף ברייטע שטײַנענדיקע וועגן.

מענטשן וועלן שווײַגנדיק בײַ די שוועלן שטיין,

פֿאַר מיר זיך נייגנדיק.

גרויסע ווײַסע פֿייגל וועלן נידעריק פֿליען,

די אַקסלען מײַנע שטרײַכנדיק.

מלאכים וועלן ערנסט און שטראָאלנדיק מיר אַנטקעגנקומען,

פֿירן מיך אַ לויטערע, אַ פֿרײַדיקע,

אַ פֿרײַדיקע, פֿאַרבלוטיקטע.

3

איך האָב בלויז איין קלייד.

עס איז אַ וואָלוול וואָלן קלייד.

דעריבער ציר איך זיך פֿאַר מײַן געליבטן

אין שוואַרצן סאַמעט פֿון טרויער.

און ווערטער שטײַנענדיקע, טרויימענדיקע, דרימלענדיקע

מורמלען ווי אַ לאַנגע פּערלקייט.

222

if I were a queen,

and you my page.

2

Your words are stones.

Your words are whips.

Blood streams.

I will close my eyes.

Soon I will be in a quiet land.

I will walk along broad gleaming roads.

People will stand on their doorsteps,

bowing silently before me.

Great white birds will fly low,

stroking my shoulders.

Angels will approach, formal and radiant,

And lead me, pure and joyful,

Joyful and bloodied.

3

I have only one dress.

A cheap woollen dress.

So I adorn myself for my beloved

in the black velvet of sorrow.

And in shimmering, dreamy, mesmerizing words,

whispering like a long string of pearls.

אָבער איך האָב בלויז איין קלייד —
פֿון ווייכן שוואַרצן סאַמעטענעם טרויער.

But I only have one dress—

of soft black velvety sorrow.

דאָס ליד פֿון אַ מיידל

יענע שעה, יענעם רגע, וועל איך אייביק געדענקן,
ווי אָן ווערטער אַ ליד, ווי אַ ליד פֿון ווערלען.
איך האָב אַזוי מורא טאָמער הער איך אויף בענקען.
ווּ ביסטו דען?

ווי צוויט אינעם ווינט האָבן געפֿלאַטערט געזיכטער
מיט צוקנדע ליפן, ווי ווּנדן רויט.
און ס'האָבן די פֿידלען, ווי טרוימענדע דיכטער,
געזונגען פֿון ליבע און טויט.

און אונדזערע שאָטנס אין ריזיקע שפּיגלען
האָבן אַנטקעגנגעשמייכלט שטײף און פֿאָרנעם,
ווען אַרום דײַנע פֿיס האָט גענומען זיך וויקלען
מײַן זײַדענער טרען.

אַ, שיינער, איך וויל ווײַל איצט אַזוי פֿיל דיר שענקען.
צי ליבע? צי טויט? ווייס איך עס דען?
נאָר עס בײַבט מיך, עס וויגט מיך, ווי שטורעם, אַ בענקען.
קום און פֿאַרברען.

226

THE SONG OF A GIRL

That time, that excitement, I will always remember,

like a song without words, like a poem by Verlaine.

I'm so afraid that if I stop yearning—

where would you be then?

Faces fluttered like blossoms in the wind,

with quivering lips like flaming wounds.

And violins, like dreamy poets,

sang of love and death.

Our shadows in giant mirrors

smiled back at us, stiff and distinguished,

as around your feet began to wind

my silken train.

Oh, handsome one, I want to give you so much now.

Love? Death? Do I know?

But it bends me, it cradles me like a storm, this yearning.

Come and burn.

א פֿרוי זאָגט

האָסט דען ניט געזען עס אין זײַן בליק און גאַנג?

ער איז גרויזאַם און גרויס,

ער איז געפֿורעמט פֿון שטורעם.

די וועלט איז פֿאַר זײַן אימפעטיקן גאַנג

אַ צו ענג הויז.

און פֿאַר די שפֿורן

פֿון זײַנע פֿלאַמענדיקע טריט

בין איך די טרויערדיקע ערד, שוואַרץ און מיד.

זעסט ניט די ווּנדן פֿון די שאַרפֿע שפֿורן?

אָבער אַ מאָל

בין איך פֿון קינדער-מעשׂהלעך דער הויכער טורעם

און שיץ אים, אַ דערשראָקענעם, פֿון שטורעם.

228

A WOMAN SAYS

Didn't you see it in his glance and his ways?

He is huge and cruel.

He is fashioned by the storm.

Beneath his emphatic tread, the world

is an overcrowded house.

And in the tracks

of his flaming steps

I am the sorrowful earth, black and weary.

Can't you see the wounds in the sharp tracks?

But once

I was the high tower of children's stories

and protected him, the frightened one, from the storm.

אַנטראַקט

דאָס איידעלע געוועב פֿון קלוגן שמואס,

ווי שפּינוועבס דורכגעציטערט פֿון אַ ווינד,

האָט פּלוצעם זיך צעריסן.

זיך וווּנדערנדיק, געלאָסן שמייכלענדיק,

האָט זי דורך דעם שווער רוישנדיקן שווייגן

דערפֿילט אים,

ווי מען פֿילט אין שלאָף אַ מאָל אַ וואָלף:

מיט אויגן גאָלדענע, פֿאַרלאָפֿענע,

ריפֿן אײַנגעצויגענע,

לאָפּעס שטײַף געבויגענע,

אין רינגען שווינדלענדע זיך דרייענדיק

אַלץ ענגער אַרום איר.

זיך וווּנדערנדיק, געלאָסן שמייכלענדיק,

מיט עקל און מיט זיסן שוידער

האָט זי דערפֿילט דעם טעם פֿון וואָלפֿיש בלוט

צווישן די ציין.

און האָט זיך לאַנגזאַם אײַנגעבויגן,

געוויזן אים דעם הייסן, דעם פֿאַרחלשטן

ווײַסל פֿון די אויגן,

אַזוי זיך לאַנגזאַם אײַנגעבויגן

און אויפֿגעקליבן

די פֿײַן געשניצטע ווערטער פֿון דעם קילן שמואס.

230

ENTRE'ACTE

The delicate weave of clever talk,

like spiderwebs tossed by the wind,

was suddenly torn.

Bemused, smiling easily,

through the heavy clatter of silence

she feels him,

the way you sometimes sense a wolf in your sleep:

with brimming, golden eyes,

ribs taut,

paws tensely poised,

rings turning dizzily

ever tighter around her.

Bemused, smiling easily,

with disgust and sweet horror

she tastes the wolfish blood

between her teeth.

Slowly she crouches,

showing him the hot, half-faint

whites of her eyes.

Oh so slowly, she crouches

and gathers up

the finely sharpened words of the cool talk.

אויף א באלקאן

פֿון װײַטן זומער פֿליט צו מיר א הייס געלעכטער

פֿון צװיי קלײנע צאַרטע פֿרױען.

זיי בלעטערן א בילדערבוך.

זייערע הענט באַגעגענען זיך אין בענקשאַפֿט.

די װײכע אַקסלען זוכן זיך און צוקן.

איבער א דאַרשטיקער אָראַנזשן־רױטער לאַנדשאַפֿט

װעלבן זיך פֿאַרװױרט די העלע לײַבער.

איבער זיי טורעמט מעכטיק א מאַן

מיט שװערע גראַציע,

װי א פּרעכטיקע און איבעריקע דעקאָראַציע.

232

ON A BALCONY

From a distant summer hot laughter floats toward me

from two small and dainty women

leafing through a picture book.

Their hands meet in longing.

Soft shoulders searching, quivering.

Over a thirsty, orange-red landscape

the bright bodies leap in confusion.

A man towers powerfully over them

with heavy grace,

like a grand and superfluous decoration.

מײַן װענוס טראָגט זײדענע שיכלעך

מײַן װענוס טראָגט זײדענע שיכלעך

אױף די בלענדנדע נאַקעטע פֿיס.

איר שױס איז אַ פֿורפֿורנע איריס

אירע היפֿטן ברײט און פֿרעצײז.

פֿון צװישן בראָנדזענע האָר

אין מורמלענדן כאָר

שלײכן זיך פּערל און ציטערן

און קושן די לענגלעכע בריסט.

אין די בלײכע לירישע ליפֿן

איז שװערמוט און גלוט.

און בליץ אין די אױגן,

נעפֿל, רױך,

פֿאַרשאָטנט װײך

פֿון גרױסן שװאַרצן באַפֿעדערטן הוט.

234

MY VENUS WEARS SILK SLIPPERS

My Venus wears silk slippers
on her glamourous bare feet.
Her lap is a crimson iris.
Her hips are broad and defined.
From her bronze hair
pearls stream and quiver
in a whispering chorus
kissing her oblong breasts.
On her pale, lyrical lips—
melancholy and ardor.
And in her eyes,
lightning, fog, smoke,
softly shadowed
by a broad, black-feathered hat.

װען צעוס, און פֿעבוס, און פֿאַן,

און קיפֿריד, זילבער־פֿיסיקע האַרין,

װעלט־באַרױשערין, װעלט־באַשיצערין

זײַנען אין שװײַגן פֿאַרהילט

אַראָפֿ פֿון אָלימפֿ,

האָבן זײ אין זײער לאַנגן און ליכטיקן גאַנג

דורך פֿלאַקערנדע און לאַנגזאַם זיך לעשנדע דורות

פֿאַקלען געצונדן און טעמפּלען געבױט

אין די הערצער פֿון אײנזאַמע,

װאָס ברענגען זײ אַלץ נאָך קרבנות און רײכערן קטורת.

די װעלט איז טיף און העל,

און ס'רױשן אײביק אַלטע װינטן דורך די יונגע בלעטער.

מיט שרעק הער איך אין מײַן זעל

די שװערע טריט פֿון פֿאַרגעסענע געטער.

236

FORGOTTEN GODS

When Zeus, Phoebus, Pan,

and Cyprian, silver-footed mistress,

animator and protector of the world,

came down from Olympus

wrapped in silence

on their long and bright route

through flaring and slowly dying generations,

they lit torches and built temples

in the hearts of the lonely,

who still bring sacrifices and burn incence.

The world is deep and bright,

and the eternal ancient winds still rustle young leaves.

Awesomely, in my very soul I hear

the heavy tread of forgotten gods.

איר שמייכל

איר שמייכל איז האַרבסטליכט איבער איר וועלט —
קיל און מיד און באַהעלט
די פּראַצע אין שטוב, די יאָרן אין שפּאַן
און מיט קינד און מאַן
דעם אייביקן נאַיוון דיאַלאָג.

דאָס איז ביי טאָג.

אָבער ביי נאַכט, אין שלאָף פֿאַרשלאָסן,
איז איר פּנים פֿרעמד. אין גראָבן ליוונטענעם העמד
טאַנצט זי אַצינד אין שענק מיט זעלנער און מאַטראָסן,
געשליידערט און צוריקגעכאַפֿט פֿון שטורעמדיקע הענט.
און לויערנדיקע אויגן אין איר איינגעזויגן,
קעפּ ווי ביי די אָקסן שטייף אַראָפּגעבויגן,
אָפּצאַסן שטאַמפֿנדיקע, אַקסלען, עלנבויגנס
ווירבלען אַרום איר אַלץ דראַענדיקער, ענגער, ציינער בליצן,
ציינער גיריק אין די ליפֿן איינגעביסן.
דאָ גאָרט דאָס בלוט זיך צו פֿאַרגיסן
און ליבע איז דאָ ענלעך צו אַ שלאַכט.

און ליבע איז אַ טשאַדענדיקער פֿאַקל, מאַכט
אומהיימלעך און בלוטנדיק די וועגן, כּישופֿט אויס
פֿון נאַכט אַ שטאָט באַרבאַרישע, אַ גאַס, אַ הויז,

238

HER SMILE

Her smile is autumnal over her world—
cool, weary and withdrawn,
the toil of the house, the years in harness,
and with husband and child
the eternal, naive dialogue.

That is daytime.

But at night, locked in sleep,
her face is alien. In a thick linen nightshirt
she dances in the tavern now with soldiers and sailors,
tossed to and fro by turbulent hands.
Lurking eyes suck her in,
ox-like heads, stiffly bent,
heels stomping, shoulders, elbows
whirling around her menacing, closer, teeth flashing
greedy, teeth biting into lips.
Here blood strives to spill itself
here, love is like a slaughter.

And love is a toxic flame that makes
the roads weird and bloody. It conjures up
a barbarous city of night, a street, a house,

מיידלעך אין אַ רינג,

און זי אין מיטן, ברוין און גרינג.

און לאַנגזאַם רירן אָן אירע רויז געפֿאַרבטע פֿינגער

דער פֿרײַנדינס קליינע אויפֿגעשפּיצטע ברוסט,

פֿאַלן צו, בלײַבן שטיין

אין גליק ביז צום פֿאַרגיין.

און גליק, געזאַנג, געוויין

איז אין דער הינגעבונג פֿון הייסע פֿינגער.

און שמערצלעך פֿלאַטערן אויף די ווײַעס

אויף אַ געזיכט, ווי פֿון אַ גאַט פֿאַרשטיינט.

ווי אַ שיינע ווילדע מעשׂה, וואָס מען האָט געלייענענט

און ניט דערלייענט, און אין מיטן זיך פֿאַרטראַכט

וועגן אַ שטאָלענער פֿיִערלעכער נאַכט,

וואָס האַלט דעם לעצטן סוד אין שויס,

ווז אַלע מעשׂיות זינען אויס —

אַזוי זעט זי איר לעבן. ווי אַ הויכן פֿלאַם,

פֿאַרשטאַרט אין גאָלדענעם טאַנץ, און ס'איז אַ טויטער פֿלאַם.

און ס'איז גרויער ווינט און גרויער ים,

און פֿון אָוונטרויט ראָלט דאָס טרויעריקע גאָלד,

און זי גייט פֿון פֿרייד באַפֿרײַט

צו לעצטער פּלאַסטיקער אײַנזאַמקייט,

און ווייסט ניט, אַז איינער וואַכט נעבן איר.

girls in a circle,

she in the centre, tanned and jaunty.

Slowly, her rosepainted fingernails touch

her girlfriend's small, pointed breast

and fall away, remain still

and happy until they pass.

And joy, song, lamentation

are in the devotion of hot fingers.

And eyelashes painfully flutter

on a face made stony as a god's.

She saw her life as

a wild and pretty story one has read

but not finished and in the middle became distracted

about a steely, solemn night,

which holds the last mystery in the lap,

where all stories end—

Like a lofty flame,

frozen stiffly in the golden dance, a dead flame.

Grey wind and grey sea,

and out of the red evening rolled the sad gold,

liberated from joy, she goes

to the last frosty solitude,

not knowing that nearby, someone is watching.

איר געזיכט איז פֿאַר אים אַ פֿאַרשלאָסענע טיר,

און הינטער איר לויערן שרעקן. ער קוקט און לײדט.

ער לײדט.

זײנע ליפֿן וועקן איר זעל אויף די טונקעלע וועגן,

אירע ליפֿן, וועלכע אין חלום זיך רעגן.

זי עפֿנט לאַנגזאַם די אויגן,

לאַנגזאַם שמייכלט זי דעם מאַן אַנטקעגן

און קומט פֿון זייער ווײט.

242

Her face is a locked door for him,

behind which fear lurks. He looks and suffers.

He suffers.

His lips rouse her soul from darkened roads,

her lips quiver in dream.

Slowly, she opens her eyes,

slowly, she smiles at her husband

and returns from a great distance.

צווישן קינעזישע לאַמטערנס

צווישן קינעזישע לאַמטערנס אין איסט-סײַדער רעסטאָראַן
שװעבן זײ אױס אַ בלעטל נאָך אַ בלעטל פֿון ראָמאַן.
בײדע אומבאַװעגלעך, קײלעכדיק און בלאַס,
װי צװײ בודאַס מיטל-יעריקע.
זי פֿליכטיק אין דעם שפּיגל: "װען ס'זאָל אַ נס געשען,
און מײַן שײנקײט קערט זיך אום װי פֿלאַם דורך עלפֿנבײן..."
דער שפּיגל ענטפֿערט: "ביסט ניט שײן".
זי שמײכלט. דער שמײכל איז אָן פֿרײד.
און די הענט ציען אױס זיך רױִק, ברײט,
נאָר אַ קלײן אָדערל אין זײ אַלץ צוקט.
און זי קוקט און קוקט,
װי ער ציט אַרױף אױף זיך די גרױע מאַסקע פֿון געדולד
און אױף די שװאַכע ליפֿן אַ שװאַכן שמײכל פֿון שולד.
אָבער איז ער שולדיק דען, װאָס ער איז ער?
װײַט ניט קײן העלד. ער װאָלט געזאָגט: ניט קײן קאַװאַליער.
אַ בעל-מטופל מיט אַ שלאַק אַ װײַב.
פֿאַרבענקט זיך נאָך אַ יום-טוב. נאָך אַ ליכטיק לײַב
און זיך פֿאַרדרײט. און װװ איז זי, די פֿרײד?
קײן מאָל ניט געװען, װי װײַט ער קען געדענקען.
און איז ער שולדיק, אַז אפֿשר דאַרף ער איצט ניט מער,
װי "טײַמס" צום פֿרישטיק, טאָסט און טשיקען צו דער צײַט,
אַ ביסל אײנזאַמקײט,
אַ שמואס מיט פֿרײַנד פֿון זײַן קרײַז און זײַן דור

244

AMONG THE CHINESE LANTERNS

In the East Side restaurant, among the Chinese lanterns

their silence speaks like the leafed pages of a novel.

Both of them motionless, round and pale,

like two middle-aged Buddhas.

She, fleetingly, in the mirror: "if a miracle happened

and my beauty returned like a flame through ivory . . ."

The mirror replied: "You are not beautiful."

She smiles. A joyless smile.

And her hands extend calmly, broadly,

only a small vein keeps quivering.

And she stares and stares

as he draws upon himself the grey mask of patience,

on his weak lips a wan smile of guilt.

But should he be blamed for being what he is?

Far from a hero. He would have said: not a cavalier

but a man burdened with children and a shrewish wife.

Longing for a holiday, for a bright body—

confusing himself. Where is she, the joy?

Never was, as far as he can remember.

But is it his fault, if perhaps now he needs only

the *Times* with breakfast, toast and chicken promptly,

a little solitude,

needs conversation with friends of his generation

מיט אַלע קלוגע ווערטלעך פֿון פֿאַר אַכצן יאָר?

און איז ער שולדיק, אויב ער מאַכט איצטער די אויגן צו

אויס מורא פֿאַרן שטורעם אין איר רו?

זי קאָקעט, אירע שמאַלע אויגן ווערן מידער, מידער,

זי האָט אים פֿײַנט. ער איז איר דערווידער.

ווי גוט, וואָס זי קען שווײַגן האַרט דורך שטונדן.

וואָס דען — אויפֿרײַסן די ווונדן?

זאָלן בעסער קרייצן זיך די בליקן,

ווי פֿאַרזשאַווערטע קינזשאַלן,

וואָס קענען אַפֿילו רעכט ניט ווײ טאָן,

און זאָלן גלייכגילטיקע ווערטער פֿאַלן

מיטן גרילץ פֿון קייטן.

אַלץ בעסער ווי צו וואַרפֿן: "זע, וואָס דו האָסט געטאָן.

האָסט מיך פֿאַרלענדט מיט צערטלענדיקע הענט,

האָסט מיך צעשטערט מיט דײַנע שוואַכע הענט,

אַרעמער, זע…"

און דאָך, און דאָך… געוועזן פֿרײד, געווען.

האָבן זיי דען ניט געהערט די אָרגלען פֿון ליבע

אונטערן אַקאָמפֿאַנימענט פֿון טויט?

און האָט דאָס אויפֿגעפֿײַטשטע בלוט

דען ניט געבענטשט די רוט

אין די הענט פֿון אַלע קלוגע לאַכער?

און יענער פֿיבער, יענער גלאַנץ פֿון זומערדיקע גערטנער,

און פֿיבער און גלאַנץ אַרום די אײנפֿאַכע ווערטער:

"מײַן ליבער."

246

with all those clever quips of eighteen years ago?

And is he guilty if now he closes his eyes

out of fear of the storm after her calm?

She stares. Her narrowing eyes become wearier, wearier.

She hates him. He is repugnant to her.

How commendable that she can be staunchly silent for hours.

What then—lacerate the wounds?

Better to cross glances

like rusted daggers

that can't wound properly,

and let indifferent words fall

with the harshness of chains.

Still better than to reproach: "See what you've done.

You've annihilated me with tender hands,

you've destroyed me with your weak hands,

pitiful one, look . . ."

And yet, and yet . . . there was joy, there was.

Didn't they hear the music of love

under the accompaniment of death?

Did the aroused blood

not bless the whip

in the hands of the clever mockers?

And that frenzy, that shimmer of summer gardens,

and the frenzy and shimmer around those simple words:

"my beloved."

און האָבן זיי...

דער קעלנער שלאָגט באַרעמהאָרציק איבער:

"װיל די לײדי קאַװע אָדער טײ?"

And have they. . .

the waiter interrupts mercifully:

"Would the lady like coffee or tea?"

ער: מאַדאַם, עס טוט מיך לייד

צו זאָגן אײַך אַזוינס, וואָס איז ניט ליב צו הערן.

איך קום, אַ פרעמדער, פון דער ווײַט

דעם פרידן אײַך צו שטערן.

זי: און אויב כ'וועל אײַך פאַרווערן?

ער: וועל איך אײַך פאָלגן און וועל אפשר דאַנקען.

צי גלייבט איר ניט, אַז איך באַדוייער

צו זײַן אַמבאַסאַדאָר פון טרויער?

נאָר ווען מען איז פון נאָענסטן פרײַנד געשיקט

און פון אַ קראַנקן...

זי: ער איז קראַנק? ער ליגט?

געשיקט מיך רופֿן? קומט.

ער: איך וויל אײַך זאָגן און איך ווער פאַרשטומט,

מאַדאַם. ער רופֿט אײַך ניט.

זי: אָ...

ער: איך ווייס,

אַז פֿרער איז יעדע טרייסט.

(פֿאַרנייגט זיך טיף)

250

HE BRINGS SORROW

He: Madam, it distresses me

    to tell you what is not pleasant to hear.

    I come, a stranger from afar

    to disrupt your happiness.

She: And were I to stop you?

He: Then I will obey you and perhaps thank you,

    will you believe that I regret

    being an ambassador of sorrow?

    But when one is sent by a close friend

    who is ill. . .

She: Is he ill? Is he in bed?

    He sent you to call me? Come!

He: I want to tell you but I am struck dumb,

    Madam, he does not call for you.

She: Oh!

He: I know

    that every consolation is presumptuous.

    (He bows deeply)

צי איז ער טאַקע ערנסט קראַנק? קען זײַן, אַז ניט.

קראַנק איז זײַן ווילן, זײַן געמיט.

דער מענטש איז שטאַרבלעך מיד...

ליגט אומבאַוועגלעך שעה נאָך שעה

מיט זײַן שמייכל פֿון האַלב פֿאַון און האַלב פּיעראַ,

מיט יענעם שמייכל צערטלעכן און רויען,

וואָס זאָגט אַזוי פֿיל צו די פֿרויען...

(כיטרע:)

אָבער דער שמייכל זאָגט צו מער,

ווי ער קען געבן...

איך זע, מײַן רעדן פֿאַלט אײַך שווער.

פֿאַרגיט מיר. אָ, איר וועט פֿאַרגעבן.

...ליגט אומבאַוועגלעך גאַנצע טעג,

ווי אַ פֿאַרחלשטער פֿון שווערן וועג,

וואָס קען ניט, וויל ניט ווײַטער גיין...

מאַדאַם, איר מעגט מיך האַלטן פֿאַר געמיין,

נאָר איך גיב איבער, וואָס ער זאָגט: "זי איז צו שיין",

זאָגט ער, און: "פֿרײַנד, קענסטו פֿאַרשטיין,

ווי שיינקייט פֿון אַ פֿינצטערן געמיט ווערט לאַסט?

אַפֿילו ווען עס איז אַ קאָסטבאַרע, אַ יום-טובֿדיקע לאַסט,

ווי אַ קעניגלעכע קרוין.

איך אָבער בין קיין קעניג ניט, נאָר איינער פֿון המון,

קענסטו פֿאַרשטיין?"

Is he so gravely ill? Perhaps only

his mood is sick, his disposition.

This person is deathly tired. . .

Lies motionless hour after hour,

his smile half fawn, half Pierrot,

with that gentle, raw smile

that promises so much to women. . .

(Slyly)

But the smile promises more,

than he can deliver. . .

I see that my words fall heavily upon you.

Forgive me. Oh, you must forgive.

. . . lies motionless entire days,

like someone half-faint after a tiring journey,

who cannot, will not, go further. . .

Madam, you may consider me vile,

but I repeat what he said: "She is too beautiful,"

he says: "Friend, can you understand,

how the beauty of a dark disposition becomes a burden?

Even when it is an expensive, a festive burden?

Like a regal crown.

But no king am I, only one of the crowd,

can you understand?"

"פֿריינד", זאָגט ער, "זאָלסט פֿון מיר ניט לאַכן:

איך בענק נאָך קליינע שפּילעוודיקע זאַכן —

נאָך ליבטן טאַנץ פֿון גראַציעזע פֿיס,

נאָך שטיפֿערישע אַריעס און געשרייען 'ביס',

נאָך יענע ביכער, ווי דאָס לעבן ווערט אַ וויץ,

און געוויס, גיווויס —

נאָך יונגע מיידלעך מיט נאַיוון חן,

וואָס מיינען 'יאָ' און זאָגן 'ניין'

און לאַכן זיך אַריין אין האַרצן..."

"זי איז צו שיין", זאָגט ער ניט דרייסט.

ער, אָרעמער אין גײַסט,

דאַרף ניט קיין קעניגרײַך.

איר זײַט פֿאַר אים צו רײַך.

"און איך, דער טויזנטפֿאַכער נאַר,

פֿאַרריייכער ווידער דעם פֿאַרלאָשענעם סיגאַר

און רעד גאַנץ וויציק, ניין? און גאַנץ געלאַסן.

און ס'עקבערט מיך די גאַנצע צײַט דער צער,

ווי קען איר אָפֿן, זי זאָל מיך ניט האַסן?"

באַגרײַפֿט איר, שיינע פֿרוי, דעם צער?

איר שווײַגט, אַ, איר זײַט שטאַלץ.

איר זײַט אַ טונקעלע סטאַטוע פֿון עבנהאָלץ,

ניין, פֿון בראָנדז.

"Friend", he says, "don't mock me:

I long for only small, playful things—

for the easy dance of graceful feet,

for mischievous arias and shouts of 'encore,'

for those books wherein life becomes a jest,

and surely, surely —

for young girls with naive charm,

who mean 'yes' but say 'no'

and laugh up their sleeves . . ."

"She is too beautiful", he says, not boldly—

he, poor in spirit,

needs no kingdom.

You are too expensive for him.

"And I, the thousand-fold fool,

re-light my cigar once again

and speak quite wittily, no? And quite easily.

But all the while, grief digs into me,

how can I hope that she won't hate me?"

Lovely lady, can you comprehend the sorrow?

You are silent. Oh, you are proud.

You are a dark statue of ebony.

No, of bronze.

ווי עס פֿאַרגייט אין שלאָף אַ העסלעכער קאָשמאַר,

אַזוי וועל איך אָט באַלד פֿאַר אײַך פֿאַרבײַגיין.

איך טראָג אַוועק מיט זיך אַ סוד פֿון וווּנדערלעכן שווײַגן,

אַ סוד אַרויסגעלייענט

פֿון אַ טונקעלן פּראָפֿיל, איידל און פֿאַרשטיינט.

נאָר, גאָט מײַנער! וואָס? איר וויינט?

ווער זאָל עס מיינען,

אַז אַ בראָנדזענע סטאַטוע קען וויינען.

Like a hateful nightmare that passes in sleep,

so will I now pass by you.

And carry away with me a secret of awesome silence,

a secret recited

from a dusky profile, refined and stony.

But, by God! What? You're crying?

Who would believe

that a bronze statue can weep.

SUPPLEMENT

הוספה

Hesofe

דער בריק

אין שווערן גאָלד פֿון דעם טאָג
דרימלט דער ווילאַמסבורג-בריק.
דאָס ווילדע האַרץ פֿון דער שטאָט
אָטעמט האַסטיק און מיד.

אין שווערן גאָלד פֿון דעם טאָג
איז די פֿערי אַ בלאָער אַקאָרד.
און פֿיבעריש און שאַרף
איז דער אַקאָמפּאַנימענט פֿון די קאַרס.

דאָס שווערע גאָלד פֿון דעם טאָג
בליצט צווישן אײַזערנע שטריק,
ברייט פֿאַרוואָרפֿן ווי נעצן
צו פֿאַנגען דאָס גליק.

אָבער איך וויל ניט קיין גליק.
איך וויל מײַן צער און מײַן סוד.
איך בין אַ גאָלדענע בריק
איבער דער שטאָלענער שטאָט.

THE BRIDGE

In the harsh gold of day
the Williamsburg bridge is drowsing.
The wild heart of the city
breathes hot and weary.

In the harsh gold of day
the ferryboat is a blue chord.
And feverish and sharp
is the accompaniment of the cars.

The harsh gold of day
flashes through the iron cables,
broadly cast like nets
to seize joy.

But it's not joy I seek.
I want my anguish and my mystery.
I am a golden bridge
over the steely city.

מײַן געליבטנס ליד

מיט דעם בלייכן רעגן פֿאַלן אירע ווערטער וועגן אָפּערע, דעם לעצטן
לידערבוך און וועגן דעם, צי איך ליב זי. ווי פֿײַנלעך איז אַ מאָל אַ
פֿײַנע פֿרויען-שטימע.

מײַן האַרץ איז שטיל. איך בין אַן אָטעם פֿון דעם גרויסן שווײַגן. איך
בין אַ טראָפּן אין דער גרויער נאַכט. איך בין אַ טרערער, וואָס פֿאַלט
אין אָפּגרונט פֿון דער נאַכט, אין שווײַגן.

אין דעם בלייכן רעגן וויינט די ווייכע שטימע: "צי ליב איך זי?" מײַן
ליבע, איך בין זי מיד. "איך ליב ניט מער?" אָ, איך בין מיד פֿון ליבע.
מײַן האַרץ איז שטיל.

ווי פֿײַנלעך איז אַ מאָל אַ פֿײַנע פֿרויען-שטימע.

MY LOVER'S POEM

Her words fall along with the dull rain, about opera, the latest book of poetry and whether I love her. How painful sometimes is the fine voice of a woman.

My heart is still. I am a breath of the great silence. I am a drop in the grey night. I am a tear that falls in the abyss of night, silently.

In the dull rain, the soft voice weeps: "Do I love her?" My love, I'm weary.
"I don't love you anymore?" Oh, I'm weary of love.
My heart is still.

How painful sometimes is the fine voice of a woman.

פֿאַר נאַכט אין פּאַרק

די שעה שפּילט איצט אויף שטילסטע פֿלייטן.
אַפֿילו צערטלעכקייט קאָן ווי טוון.

ס'איז אָוונטרווייט.
די שעה פֿון ליבשאַפֿט, און פֿון אויפֿלײַכטן, פֿון בעטן.

מײַן שוועסטער, מיידל, קיל און שלאַנק,
איך בין אויך געוואָרן דופֿט, און ווינט און געזאַנג.

און דו, וואָס דו שמייכלסט מיד און פֿויל,
אָ, קען איך דאָס צוקן פֿון דײַן טרויעריקן מויל.

די שעה שפּילט איצט אויף שטילסטע פֿלייטן.

יענע טראַגישע מאַסקע, דאָס פּנים פֿון מאָן,
גייט מיר נאָך ווי אַ קללה, שפּאָן נאָך שפּאָן.

און דער קריפּל הינקט מיר אַנטקעגן, גלייב איך, יאָרן לאַנג.
זײַ מוחל מיר, ברודער, וואָס גליך איז מײַן גאַנג.

ס'איז אָוונטרווייט.
די שעה שפּילט איצט אויף שטילסטע פֿלייטן.

DUSK IN THE PARK

Time plays now on the quietest of flutes.
Even tenderness can wound.

Red glow of evening.
The time for love, for radiance, for entreaty.

My sister, girlish, cool and slender,
I too was fragrance, wind and song.

And you who smile wearily and lazily,
oh, how I know that quiver of your sad mouth.

Time plays now on the quietest of flutes.

That tragic mask, the face of a man,
follows me step by step like a curse.

And it seems the cripple always limps towards me
pardon me, brother, for walking straight.

Red glow of evening
Time plays now on the quietest of flutes.

צום נאָנטן און צום ווײַטן בין איך צוגעשמידט מיט קייטן.

אָ, שטילער, שטילער, יעדער ריר קאָן קוי טון.

To the nearest and furthest I am welded by chains.

Oh, quietly, quietly, each stir can wound.

מײַנע טעג װאָרצלען אין שטײַנער

מײַנע טעג װאָרצלען אין שטײַנער.
װאָקסן טוט אזױ װײ.
נאָר אַלץ פֿאַרגײַסטיקער, רײַנער
איז די בלויקייט איבער זײ.

װי מיט דינע פֿאַרקריפלטע צװײַגן.
זײ װאָלטן אַ הימל געשפֿינט
איבער מיר, איבער מײַן שװײַגן,
װאָס װײלט דאָ אַ װײַל און פֿאַרשװינדט.

MY DAYS TAKE ROOT IN STONES

My days take root in stones.

Growing causes so much pain.

But the blueness above them

is altogether more ethereal, purer.

As with slender, gnarled branches

which tarries a while and is gone

they would weave a heaven

over me, and over my silence.

שיכור פֿון ביטערן אמת

דאָס טונקעלע, שווערע — איך נעם עס.

קום און שלאָג און פֿאַרוווּנד, ווילדע פּײַן.

שיכור פֿון ביטערן אמת,

שטויס איך אָפּ יעדן אַנדערן ווײַן.

דאָס טונקעלע, שווערע, פֿאַרברויכטע,

וואָס פֿאַרשעמט מיך טאָג אויס און טאָג אײַן,

וועל איך דורכגלוטן, דורכבלוטן, דורכלויכטן,

פֿאַרוואַנדלען אין איידלסטן שײַן.

פֿון דעם טונקעלן, שווערן און האַרטן,

ווי אין דינסט פֿון אַ הויכן געבאָט,

בעת איך ליכטיקע טרעפּ צום געגאַרטן,

טרוימענדן, שטראַלנדן גאָט.

270

DRUNK FROM THE BITTER TRUTH

The dark and the heavy—I take them.

Come strike and wound, wild anguish.

Drunk from the bitter truth,

I refuse all other wine.

The dark, the heavy, the used up

shame me day in, day out,

I will burn them through, bleed them through, blaze them forth,

and transform them into the most delicate glow.

From the dark, the heavy and the hard,

as if in service to a higher command,

I build luminous steps to the sought-after,

dreaming and radiant God.

זי מיט די קאַלטע מאַרמאָרנע בריסט

זי מיט די קאַלטע מאַרמאָרנע בריסט

און מיט די שמאָלע ליכטיקע הענט,

זי האָט איר שיינקייט פֿאַרשווענדט

אויף מיסט, אויף גאָרנישט.

זי האָט עס אפֿשר געוואָלט, אפֿשר געגלוסט

צו אומגליק, צו זיבן מעסערס פֿון פּײַן

און פֿאַרגאָסן דעם לעבנס הייליקן ווײַן

אויף מיסט, אויף גאָרנישט.

איצט ליגט זי מיט אַ צעבראָכן געזיכט.

דער געשענדטער גײַסט פֿאַרלאָזט די שטײַג.

פֿאַרבײַגייער, האָב רחמונות און שווײַג —

זאָג גאָרנישט.

272

SHE OF THE COLD MARBLE BREASTS

She of the cold marble breasts
and the slender, light hands—
she squandered her beauty
on rubbish, on nothing.

Perhaps she wanted it, perhaps lusted after it:
the unhappiness, the seven knives of anguish
to spill life's holy wine
on rubbish, on nothing.

Now she lies with shattered face.
Her ravaged spirit has abandoned its cage.
Passerby, have pity, be silent—
say nothing.

איך וויל דיר, דעם בייזן און דעם צאַרטן

איך וויל דיר, דעם בייזן און דעם צאַרטן,
דערצײילן, ווי מײַן איז געווען
פֿון שטענדיק אָן אויף שפּיץ פֿינגער אַ וואַרטן.
אויף ליבע? ניט אויף ליבע. נײן.

נאָר אויף אַ ווונק, אַ נס, אַ שטים,
ווי אָטעם נאָנט און דאָך ווייט ווי אַ שטערן,
אויף יענעם יובלענדיקן רוף, וואָס אים
מיט צוגעמאַכטע אויגן קאָן מען בלויז דערהערן.

און האָב דאָך ליב די ערד, די רחבֿות און דעם חן
פֿון פּראָסטן זײַן, די ליבע זינד, די וואָר די האַרטע.
און דאָך, און דאָך — דאָס גאַנצע לעבן איז געווען
אַ האָרכן, אויף די שפּיץ פֿינגער אַ וואַרטן.

274

I WANT, ANGRY AND TENDER ONE

I want, angry and tender one,

to tell you how it was with me,

always waiting on tiptoe.

For love? Not for love. No.

Just for a hint, a miracle, a voice—

close as a breath, yet distant as a star,

for the jubilant call that can be heard

only with closed eyes.

And yet, I love the earth, the breadth and charm

of ordinary life, its beloved sins, its harsh reality.

And yet, and yet—all my life was

anticipation, a waiting on tiptoe.

bibliography

Books in English

Akhmatova, Anna. *Poems*. New York: W. W. Norton, 1983.

Baskin, Judith R., ed. *Jewish Women in Historical Perspective*. Detroit: Wayne State University Press, 1991.

————. *Women of the Word*. Detroit: Wayne State University Press, 1994.

Barnstone, Aliki, and Willis Barnstone, eds. *A Book of Women Poets*. New York: Schocken Books, 1980.

Barnstone, Willis. *The Poetics of Translation: History, Theory, Practice*. New Haven: Yale University Press, 1993.

Baum, Charlotte, Paula Hyman, and Sonya Michel. *The Jewish Woman in America*. New York: Dial Press, 1976.

Blake, William. *The Portable Blake*. New York: The Viking Press, 1946.

Dawidowicz, Lucy. *The Golden Tradition*. Boston: Beacon Press, 1967.

Donoghue, Denis. *The Ordinary Universe*. London: Faber and Faber, 1968.

Falk, Marcia. *Introduction: Malca Heifetz Tussman*. Detroit: Wayne State University Press, 1992.

Fishman, Sylvia Barack. *Follow My Footprints*. Hanover, N.H.: Brandeis University Press, 1992.

Frye, Northrop. *Anatomy of Criticism*. Princeton: Princeton University Press, 1971.

Gilbert, Sandra M., and Susan Gubar. *The Madwoman in the Attic*. New Haven: Yale University Press, 1979.

Glanz, Rudolph. *Eastern European Jewish Women*. Vol. 2, New York: Ktav Publishing, 1976.

Glenn, Susan A. *Daughters of the Shtetl*. Ithaca: Cornell University Press, 1990.

Goldman, Emma. *Living My Life*. New York: New American Library, 1977.

Goldsmith, Emanuel S. *Modern Yiddish Culture*. New York: Shapolsky Publishers, 1987.

Greer, Germaine. *Slip-Shod Sybils*. Penguin Books, 1995.

Hapgood, Hutchins. *The Spirit of the Ghetto*. New York: Schocken Books, 1966.

Harshav, Benjamin. *The Meaning of Yiddish*. Berkeley: University of California Press, 1990.

Harshav, Benjamin, and Barbara Harshav, eds. *American Yiddish Poetry*. Berkeley: University of California Press, 1986.

Howe, Irving. *The World of Our Fathers*. New York: Harcourt Brace Jovanovich, 1976.

Howe, Irving, and Eliezer Greenberg, eds. *A Treasury of Yiddish Poetry*. New York: Holt Rinehart and Winston, 1969.

Howe, Irving, and Eliezer Greenberg. *Voices from the Yiddish: Essays, Memoirs, Diaries*. New York: Schocken Books, 1975.

Howe, Irving, Ruth R. Wisse, and Chone Shmeruk, eds. *The Penguin Book of Modern Yiddish Verse.* New York: Viking Penguin, 1987.

Kalechovsky, Robert and Roberta Kalechovsky, eds. *The Global Anthology of Jewish Women Writers.* Marblehead, Mass.: Micah Publications, 1990.

Kayser, Wolfgang. *The Grotesque in Art and Literature.* Bloomington: Indiana University Press, 1963.

Kazin, Alfred. *Introduction: The Portable Blake.* New York: Viking Press, 1960.

Klepficz, Irena. "Introduction," *Found Treasures.* Toronto: Second Story Press, 1994.

Lasker-Schuler, Else. *Hebrew Ballads and Other Poems.* Philadelphia: Jewish Publication Society of America, 1980.

Leftwich, Joseph. *Great Yiddish Writers of the Twentieth Century.* Northvale, N.J.: Jason Aronson, 1969.

Liptzin, Sol. *A History of Yiddish Literature.* New York: Jonathan David Publishers, 1985.

Madison, Charles A. *Yiddish Literature, Its Scope and Major Writers.* New York: Frederick Ungar Publishing, 1968.

Margolin, Anna. New York, YIVO Archive.

Olsen, Tillie. *Tell Me a Riddle.* New York: Dell, 1971.

Rank, Otto. *Art and the Artist.* New York: W. W. Norton, 1932.

Rudavsky, T. M., ed. *Gender and Judaism.* New York: New York University Press, 1995.

Rilke, Rainer Maria. *Neue Gedichte / New Poems* (bilingual). Translated by Stephen Cohn. Manchester, UK: Carcanet Press. 1997.

Schwartz, Howard, and Rudolf Anthony, eds. *Voices within the Ark.* New York: Avon Publishers, 1980.

Shepherd, Naomi. *A Price Below Rubies: Jewish Women as Rebels and Radicals.* Cambridge: Harvard University Press, 1993.

Sokoloff, Naomi B., Anne Lapidus Lerner, and Anita Norich, eds. *Gender and Text in Modern Hebrew and Yiddish Literature.* New York: Jewish Theological Society, 1992.

Sutzkever, A. *Selected Poetry and Prose.* Translated by Barbara and Benjamin Harshav. Berkeley: University of California Press, 1991.

Vendler, Helen. *The Music of What Happens.* Cambridge: Harvard University Press, 1988.

Venuti, Lawrence, ed. *Translation Studies Reader.* London: Routledge, 2000.

Verlaine, Paul. *One Hundred and One Poems* (bilingual). Translated by Norman R. Shapiro. Chicago: University of Chicago Press, 1999.

Waddington, Miriam. *Apartment Seven.* Toronto: Oxford University Press, 1989.

Wechsler, Robert. *Performing without a Stage: The Art of Literary Translation.* North Haven Conn.: Catbird Press, 1998.

Weinberg, Sydney Stahl. *The World of Our Mothers.* New York: Schocken Books, 1988.

Whitman, Ruth. *An Anthology of Modern Yiddish Poetry.* New York: Workmen's Circle, 1979.

Wisse, Ruth R. *A Little Love in Big Manhattan.* Cambridge: Harvard University Press, 1988.

Articles and Essays in English

Cooper, Adriennne. "About Anna Margolin," *The Tribe of Dinah.* Boston: Beacon Press, 1986. Pp. 154–159.

Falk, Marcia. "With Teeth in the Earth: The Life and Art of Malca Heifetz-Tussman." *Shofar.* Vol. 9, #4, Summer, 1991.

Hellerstein, Kathryn. "A Question of Tradition: Women Poets in Yiddish." *Handbook of Jewish-American Literature*. New York: Greenwood Press, 1988.

Noversztern, Avraham. "Who Would Have Believed That a Bronze Statue Could Weep? The Poetry of Anna Margolin." *Prooftexts*. Vol. 10, #3, 10th Anniversary Volume, Baltimore: Johns Hopkins University Press, 1990.

Pratt, Norma Fein. "Culture and Radical Politics: Yiddish Women Writers, 1890–1940," *Female, Feminine amd Feminist Images,* 1983, pp. 131–152.

———. "Introduction" to Special Edition of *Shofar*. Vol. 9, #4, Summer, 1991.

———. "Anna Margolin's Lider: A Study in Women's History, Autobiography, and Poetry," *Studies in American Jewish Literature*. Vol. 3, 1983.

Rosenfarb, Chava, *Translator's Note on Lecture,* University of Toronto, 1992.

Seller, Maxine S. "Defining Socialist Womanhood: The Women's Page of the Jewish Daily Forward," *American Jewish History*. June, 1987.

Shmeruk, Chone. "Yiddish Literature," *Encyclopedia Judaica*. Jerusalem: Keter Publishing, Vol. 16, 1971. Pp. 798–834.

Wenkart, Henny, ed. *Sarah's Daughters Sing*. Hoboken, N.J.: Ktav Publishing House, 1990.

Zucker, Sheva. "Yente Serdatzky: Lonely Lady of Yiddish Literature," *Yiddish*. Vol. 8, #2, New York, 1992.

Books, Articles and Essays in Yiddish

Ayzland, Reuven. *Fun undzer friling*. New York, 1954. Pp. 129–172.

Glatshteyn, Yankev. *In tokh genumen*. New York: Farband Book Publishing, 1956.

Korman, Ezra. *Yidishe dikhterins*. Chicago: Farlag Shtein, 1928.

Manger, Itsik. *Shriftn un proze*. Tel Aviv: Farlag I. L. Peretz, 1980.

Margolin, Anna. *Poems*. Jerusalem: Magnes Press, Hebrew University, 1991.

———. *Lider*. New York: Orion Press, 1929.

Niger, Sh. "Di lider fun Anna Margolin," *Der Tog*. New York, April, 1929.

———. "Di Yidishe literatur un di lezerin" (1929). *Bleter geshikhte fun der yidisher literatur*. New York, 1959.

Noversztern, Avraham. Anna Margolin, *Lider*. Jerusalem: Magnes Press, 1991.

———. "Anna Margolin—Materialn tsu ir poetisher geshtalt," *YIVO Bleter*. New Series, Band 1, New York, 1991 (Correspondence between Anna Margolin and Reuven Ayzland).

Ravitch, Meylekh. *Mayn leksikon*. Montreal: Northern Printing, 1945.

Segal, I. I. "Anna Margolin—Eulogy," *Zukunft*. New York, September, 1952.

Tenenboym, S. *Dikhters un doyres* (Writers and Generations) (New York, 1955).

Zucker, Sheva. "Anna Margolin un di poesia funem geshpoltenem ikh," *YIVO Bleter*. New Series, Band 1, New York, 1991.

Video

Pratt, Norma Fein. *Anna Margolin*. UCLA Educational Media Center, 1988.

index to first lines in English

index to first lines in Yiddish

דער אינדעקס צו די ערשטע ליניעס אויף ייִדיש

285

287